First Steps to Preschool Inclusion

First Steps to Preschool Inclusion

How to Jumpstart Your Programwide Plan

by

Sarika S. Gupta, Ph.D.
Johns Hopkins University
Baltimore, Maryland

with

William R. Henninger, IV, Ph.D.
University of Northern Iowa
Cedar Falls

and

Megan E. Vinh, Ph.D.
University of Oregon
Portland

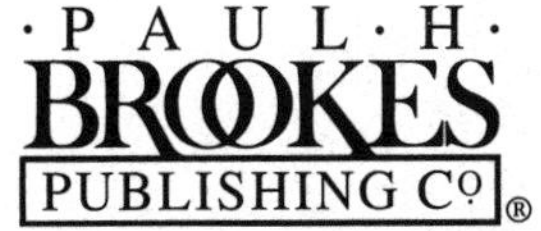

Baltimore • London • Sydney

·P A U L·H·
BROOKES
PUBLISHING CO.®

Paul H. Brookes Publishing Co.
Post Office Box 10624
Baltimore, MD 21285-0624

www.brookespublishing.com

Typeset by Scribe Inc., Philadelphia, Pennsylvania.
Manufactured in the United States of America by
Sheridan Books, Chelsea, Michigan.

The individuals described in this book are composites or real people whose situations are masked and are based on the authors' experiences. In all instances, names and identifying details have been changed to protect confidentiality.

Library of Congress Cataloging-in-Publication Data

The Library of Congress has cataloged the printed edition as follows:
Gupta, Sarika S.
First steps to preschool inclusion : how to jumpstart your programwide plan / by Sarika S. Gupta, Ph.D. with William R. Henninger, IV, Ph.D., and Megan E. Vinh, Ph.D.
pages cm
Includes index.
ISBN 978-1-59857-252-0 (pbk. : alk. paper)—ISBN 1-59857-252-0 (pbk. : alk. paper)—ISBN 978-1-59857-817-1 (epub e- book)
1. Children with disabilities—Education (Preschool) 2. Children with disabilities—Education (Early childhood) . 3. Inclusive education. 4. Special education. 5. Early childhood education—Administration. I. Henninger, William R., IV II. Vinh, Megan E. III. Title.

LC4019.2.G86 2014
371.9'046—dc23 2014012287

British Library Cataloguing in Publication data are available from the British Library.

2018 2017 2016 2015 2014

10 9 8 7 6 5 4 3 2 1

Contents

About the Forms

Purchasers of this book may download, print, and/or photocopy the blank forms for educational use. These materials are included with the print book and are also available at **www.brookespublishing.com/gupta/eforms**.

About the Authors

Sarika "Sari" S. Gupta, Ph.D., is Assistant Professor with the Center for Technology in Education with the Johns Hopkins University's School of Education. She holds a doctoral degree in special education from the University of Maryland, and she completed a postdoctoral fellowship in early childhood special education leadership and policy at the University of Colorado. Over the past 15 years, she has blended teaching, research, and policy experiences to support preschool inclusion. She taught young children (birth to 5 years old) with and without disabilities in typical and inclusive settings, coached Head Start teachers, and worked at the Office of Special Education Programs, and most recently was Assistant Professor of Early Childhood Special Education at George Mason University. She has led numerous professional development workshops focused on individualizing instruction for preschoolers with special needs and promoting young children's social and emotional outcomes. Dr. Gupta is an active member of the Division for Early Childhood (DEC) of the Council for Exceptional Children and served as their national Children's Action Network (CAN) coordinator in 2011. In 2013, she assisted in convening DEC's first leadership summit. Her research interests include leadership preparation and coaching in early childhood. She is the principal investigator for a pilot study that will explore preschool administrators' educational and programmatic needs as they pertain to inclusion.

William "Bill" Henninger, IV, Ph.D., is Assistant Professor of Family Studies at the University of Northern Iowa in the College of Social and Behavioral Sciences. He obtained his Ph.D. from Iowa State University in human development and family studies with a specialization in early childhood special education. He has also completed a postdoctoral fellowship in early childhood special education leadership and policy at the University of Colorado Denver. Prior to obtaining his Ph.D., Dr. Henninger worked for Juniper Gardens Children's Project (JGCP) in Kansas City, Kansas. JGCP is a research center affiliated with the University of Kansas that serves inner-city Kansas through early intervention research. Dr. Henninger's major research interests include social-emotional development of children and adolescents who are typical and nontypical. In his spare time, he enjoys spending time with his wife and dogs.

Megan E. Vinh, Ph.D., is an educational consultant with Technical Assistance and Consulting Services, a research and outreach unit at the University of Oregon. She provides technical assistance and consultation to states' agencies of special education (under a grant funded by the Office of Special Education Programs) to improve services for young children with disabilities and their families. She has experience with projects related to early childhood outcomes, early childhood special education, preschool inclusion, and evidence-based strategies to promote the social and emotional development of young children.

About the Authors

About the Contributor

Laura S. DiNardo, M.Ed., graduated from Kenyon College in 2010 with a B.A. in anthropology. She worked for 2 years as an instructional assistant in a preschool special education classroom before enrolling in a master's program in special education at George Mason University (GMU). She works with the GMU Learning into Future Environments program, a postsecondary program for students with intellectual and developmental disabilities.

Foreword

I must admit to some ambivalence about writing this foreword. On the one hand, I am delighted to endorse Gupta, Henninger, and Vinh's altogether timely, practical, and well-thought-out procedural guide to expanding preschool inclusion. On the other hand, the need for such a guide is a disturbing reminder of the extent to which the field does not practice inclusion. If one examines readily available data from the Annual Reports to Congress on Special Education Services issued by the Office of Special Education Programs, it is clear that the inclusion "needle" has not moved forward in more than 3 decades, and it can even be argued that some regression has occurred. This trend exists in spite of preschool inclusion studies uniformly demonstrating positive benefits for all participants. Looking more deeply at the national database, one sees glaring disparities across states, with inclusion being afforded to more than 90% of children in some areas and to less than 10% in others!

After 4 decades of federal legislation; dozens of empirical studies; hundreds of millions of dollars spent on training and technical assistance at the federal, state, and local levels; and numerous federal court cases supporting inclusive options, *First Steps to Preschool Inclusion: How to Jumpstart Your Programwide Plan* is precisely what the field needs.

In down-to-earth yet technically precise language, Gupta, Henninger, and Vinh provide the reader with all the necessary tools to expand inclusive options. These tools include 1) a precise definition and rationale for inclusion, 2) specific federal legislation and policies that support inclusion, 3) a summary of research supporting inclusion, 4) key concerns related to program readiness for inclusion, 5) considerations specific to existing program requirements and resources available, 6) strategies for supporting programwide change, and 7) ways to assess and overcome barriers.

This volume's structural aspects make it truly unique. For example, the liberal use of case examples permits the reader to directly relate the content to his or her own circumstances and challenges. The available forms will be of great use to administrators, teachers, parents, advocates, and all affected by inclusion. Similarly, the queries in each chapter provide the reader with an important review and procedural guide to relating the book's content to individual circumstances and change initiatives.

In essence, Gupta, Henninger, and Vinh have distilled all the critical elements affecting inclusion into an engaging, resource-rich, and timely volume. One can easily envision administrators inspired and confident in moving an inclusion agenda forward. Likewise, one can see parents and advocates thankful to have the legal and scientific evidence readily available to advance inclusion. Teachers and other practitioners can take heart in knowing that this work makes clear that resources and supports must be in place for inclusion to realize its full potential.

Phillip S. Strain, Ph.D.
University of Colorado Denver

Acknowledgments

It started with a team: Team Postdoc. We all moved to Denver to pursue a postdoctoral fellowship in early childhood special education leadership (ECSEL) with Barbara J. Smith. The goal of ECSEL was to prepare us as leaders to research, develop, and implement policies, systems, and program features that promote positive outcomes for young children with or at risk for delays or disabilities, for their families, and for those who work with them—no small task.

Maybe it was the sunny weather. Maybe it was the indescribably beautiful surroundings or the clear air that led us to believe we could accomplish this task so early in our careers. We suspect it was the combination of these factors at just the right time and with just the right people that gave life to this idea. In the end, we know it was encouragement from strong leadership, a value we hope we convey in this book, that helped us achieve this goal.

We sat down at The Market in Denver, Colorado, to flesh out our ideas. What was needed in the field? What important concepts needed to be addressed? What were we learning during our postdoctoral fellowship that we thought others should know and needed to know?

We are thankful to many mentors and colleagues for their support in writing this book. First, Barbara J. Smith's vision provided us with a focused course of study to understand the historical and legal factors that drove the development of the early childhood special education system we support and continuously work to improve. With colleagues Beth Rous, Phil Strain, Ritu Chopra, and Sheila Shannon, Barbara taught us how to translate research findings into policy implications and how to consider the breadth of supports needed to ensure the success of all young children.

We also thank our postdoctoral colleague, Amanda Stein, who helped us develop the vision for this book and the concrete examples in Chapter 7 that we know will help leaders work through challenges. Martha Diefendorf, Mary Louise Peters, and Debbie Cate brainstormed early versions of Chapter 5 with us, leading us to develop a resource chapter (Chapter 5) that better depicts the continuum of programs in early care and education and their requirements for inclusion. A special thanks also goes to Laura DiNardo for reviewing formatting and content as we revised chapters along the way.

We also thank our doctoral mentors Joan Lieber, Gayle Luze, Carla Peterson, and Sydney Zentall for continued support beyond our course of study and as we further this work.

Moving the content in this book to a comprehensive and complete volume was a new task for us and was possible with continued guidance and support from our Brookes Publishing colleagues Johanna Schmitter, Julie Chavez, and Sarah Zerofsky, as well as countless others. Thank you for finding ways to improve content so that it may reach a broader audience.

It has been more than 35 years since the passage of the Education for All Handicapped Children Act of 1975 (PL 94-142), but only 50% of preschoolers with disabilities nationwide are being included for more than 80% of the time in general education settings. So many before us—families, researchers, practitioners, and policy makers—worked diligently to ensure this, and to them we are grateful for beginning this challenging and rewarding work.

We hope that our commitment to continuing the good work of those before us is evident and that you will join us in supporting administrators and leaders to lead the collaborative work that teachers, families, and practitioners will depend on to meaningfully include young children with disabilities in preschool settings.

Preface: What Is the Rationale for This Book?

Sarika S. Gupta

We believe in inclusion. That, quite simply, is the rationale for this book.

First, we believe in inclusion because it supports the right of every child to participate meaningfully in "a broad range of activities and contexts as full members of families, communities, and societies" (DEC/NAEYC, 2009, p. 2).

Second, we believe in inclusion because it works! Years of research show that children—both with and without disabilities—benefit from inclusion. Parent perceptions, teacher feedback, and child outcomes suggest that children with disabilities learn positive social behaviors and academic skills from typically developing peers (see Chapter 2). Meanwhile, typically developing children develop compassion that lasts well into adolescence—and likely adulthood. Families, too, benefit as they develop greater sensitivity and learn to celebrate individual differences in their young children.

Third, we believe in inclusion because we have witnessed the benefits. I (Gupta) worked as a preschool teacher for 5 years, 2 of which were in an independent inclusive preschool program. One year, my 4-year-old classroom of 18 included 1 child with a visual impairment and several children with social and communication delays. The next year, at least one-third of the class had social and communication delays, and some of these delays were attributed to learning English as a second language. I *saw* the benefits I have described, and they were powerful. I was also fortunate to have a co-teacher and several on-site specialists help me engage parents in planning, collecting data, and monitoring children's progress. I realized quickly the value of teamwork in supporting all young children and their families and pursued my doctorate to learn about research efforts to support teachers' abilities to individualize and differentiate instruction for children who need additional support.

We three authors met during our postdoctoral fellowship in early childhood special education leadership (ECSEL) and policy. Together, we learned about the federal laws and policies that govern inclusion (e.g., Individuals with Disabilities Education Improvement Act [IDEA] of 2004, PL 108-446), how we could promote programwide change through collaboration (e.g., Hayden, Frederick, & Smith, 1997), and that programwide change takes time (e.g., Wallace, Blase, Fixsen, & Naoom, 2008). We also learned that there was little beyond what our mentors had published (e.g., Lieber et al., 1997; Peterson, Fox, & Santos, 2009; Smith & Rose, 1993; Smith, Strain, & Ostrosky, 2004; Wolery & Odom, 2000) to help early childhood leaders specifically use administrative support and collaboration as a vehicle to promote programwide inclusion. For us, deciding what to do next was easy to figure out but challenging to accomplish. We agreed there was little support for administrators and that developing a guidebook describing inclusion was an important first step. We set out to compile, summarize, translate, and blend the research into a unique and practical product to help administrators think about inclusion as an approach they could facilitate and lead.

WHAT IS INCLUSION?

Inclusion is the full participation of preschoolers with disabilities with their typically developing peers. It is supported by federal law, more than 30 years of evidence, and recommended practices in early childhood. Many preschoolers with disabilities nationwide are included in regular preschool settings, such as state-funded prekindergarten programs, child care, and Head Start programs. States report that nearly 50% of the 731,250 preschoolers with disabilities nationwide spend the majority of their time in general education settings (Lazara et al., 2011). This also means that preschoolers with disabilities are spending almost half of their time in segregated settings.

WHY ARE PRESCHOOLERS WITH DISABILITIES NOT BEING INCLUDED?

The lack of inclusion has several reasons: 1) a lack of high-quality prekindergarten classrooms (Barnett, Carolan, Fitzgerald, & Squires, 2011); 2) level funding for IDEA Part B, Section 619, meaning funding for preschool special education has not increased enough to meet the growing population of children with disabilities since 1997; and 3) despite good intentions, interests, and efforts, preschool administrators and leaders may not know how to make inclusion work.

WHO NEEDS GUIDANCE?

Anyone interested, ideally, needs guidance! Realistically, however, administrators, leaders, teachers, specialists, and parents and families can all benefit from additional guidance about inclusion, how to make it work, and how to better support children with disabilities needs. Realizing the breadth of this audience, and given our training in ECSEL and policy, we decided to focus on developing a guidebook for administrators and leaders—the individuals whom parents, families, teachers, and specialists rely on for direction and support when it comes to their child's education. Lieber and colleagues (1997) learned that, with administrative support, teachers and specialists feel more capable of including children with disabilities. Families also may be less likely to harbor negative attitudes and more likely to develop a sense of community when administrators and leaders establish policies that invite and cultivate a culture of sensitivity and respect based on family needs and child characteristics (Beckman et al., 1998).

Prekindergarten program administrators and leaders hold positions in which they can influence the policies and practices within a state, district, and/or program; however, they have multiple and sometimes competing responsibilities. They are called on to inspire, facilitate, and sustain quality improvement initiatives and tasked with the day-to-day operational duties of their programs. They must understand the growing need for evidence showing that their students are making gains. Finally, they are responsible for coordinating the inclusion of children with disabilities. These collective responsibilities may overwhelm administrators with little knowledge of child development, early childhood education (ECE), and early childhood special education (ECSE) policies and practices. In fact, a recent survey in New Jersey confirmed the need for specialized knowledge among pre-K directors. Directors desired training in administrative approaches, early childhood content, and "learning more about children with special needs" (Ryan, Whitebook, Kipnis, & Sakai, 2011, p. 11). For leaders with little knowledge of child development and ECE, including children with disabilities can feel overwhelming.

Fortunately, resources from the National Association for the Education of Young Children (NAEYC) and the Division for Early Childhood (DEC) of the Council for Exceptional Children can assist pre-K leaders in developing high-quality inclusive environments (e.g., Sandall, Hemmeter, Smith, & McLean, 2005). Unfortunately, only a handful of research summaries (e.g., National Professional Development Center on Inclusion, 2009), books (Smith &Rose, 1993; Wolery & Odom, 2000), and policy briefs (Gupta, 2011; Smith, Strain, & Ostrosky, 2004) advise administrators and leaders on how to build the capacity and culture for inclusion daily. Based on how little information there is, we argue that there is a need to provide early childhood administrators and leaders with explicit guidance on what inclusion is, what it entails, and tips to ensure a successful start-up effort.

WHAT IS THE PURPOSE OF THIS GUIDEBOOK?

The purpose of this book is to provide administrators and leaders with the foundational knowledge needed to, first, understand preschool inclusion and, second, build the collaborative work force to implement it.

WHO SHOULD READ THIS GUIDEBOOK?

Primarily early childhood administrators, early childhood leaders, and aspiring leaders would benefit most from this book. Early childhood administrators may encompass a range of roles, such as preschool–12 superintendents, elementary school principals, or directors of a child care center. These people are employed in positions in which they are involved with the business of operating a school system, a district, or a program. Early childhood leaders, by contrast, are professionals who coordinate inclusion efforts or serve as consultants to school systems, districts, and/or programs. For example, superintendents may hire leaders to supervise inclusion across several state prekindergarten programs. Leaders might advise administrators and teachers on the use of evidence-based practices, coordinate inclusive placements, or coach and supervise on how best to meet children's individualized needs. Finally, we envision aspiring leaders as those individuals enrolled in administrator or teacher licensure programs, teacher preparation programs, and/or state or local leadership academies and professional development events.

HOW IS THIS GUIDEBOOK ORGANIZED?

This book is set up to help you understand inclusion, prepare for inclusion, and build the capacity to include children with disabilities in your program. The book is organized into two sections: Section I: Inclusion, Policy, and Research and Section II: Critical Considerations for Inclusion.

Section I includes Chapters 1–3. It opens with an overview of inclusion and what it looks like in practice. A history of inclusion is presented in Chapter 2, along with the relevant federal legislation that supports inclusion. Chapter 3 is a summary of the benefits both children with disabilities and typical children experience as a result of inclusion; researchers have discovered both short- and long-term effects.

Section II comprises Chapters 4–7 and advises readers to systematically assess their programs; build critical partnerships with staff, families, and others; and develop a plan to implement inclusion. Chapter 4 presents resources to assess program readiness for inclusion. In addition to including strategies and resources to help you assess the physical environment of your program and individual classrooms, this chapter summarizes the hesitations that staff and families are likely to express and strategies to gain their support.

Chapter 5 describes a range of early learning programs and reviews their requirements for inclusion as well resources to help you understand them. Although inclusion is supported broadly by federal policies such as the IDEA of 2004 (PL 108-446) and the Americans with Disabilities Act of 1990 (ADA; PL 101-336), it is also supported by program requirements, such as the Head Start 10% enrollment policy.

Recognizing inclusion as a collaborative process (this is emphasized throughout the book) and as a means to lead program change efforts is addressed in Chapter 6. Finally, Chapter 7 presents commonly reported challenges related to inclusion to help you brainstorm potential solutions and strategies.

The content of each chapter is based on research and translated into everyday language. Each chapter contains practical strategies to help leaders develop and cultivate an inclusive mind-set and approach in preschool settings. We authors draw from several bodies of literature, including inclusion practices and outcomes, collaborative teaming, adult learning, tiered instruction, implementation science, and systems building to offer readers concrete, effective strategies that will enable leaders to build the infrastructure—that is, program supports—needed to include young children with disabilities.

WHAT WILL I LEARN BY READING THIS GUIDEBOOK?

You will learn a great deal about inclusion, the laws that govern it, the research that supports it, and the critical environmental and collaborative considerations needed to launch an inclusive program. At the same time, however, think of this guidebook as a starting point to understanding inclusion—the what, when, why, and how—and the leadership principles and strategies that will support its success.

WHAT THIS BOOK DOES NOT DO . . .

This guidebook does not provide instructional strategies for teachers to support children in classroom settings. Here are several online and print resources that may be helpful in this regard.

Online Resources

- Center for Social Emotional Foundations for Early Learning (CSEFEL): http://csefel.vanderbilt.edu/
- Center for Response to Intervention in Early Childhood (CRTIEC): http://www.crtiec.dept.ku.edu/
- CONNECT: Center to Mobilize Early Childhood Knowledge: http://community.fpg.unc.edu/
- Head Start Center for Inclusion: http://depts.washington.edu/hscenter/
- National Professional Development Center on Inclusion (NPDCI): http://npdci.fpg.unc.edu/
- Technical Assistance Center on Social Emotional Intervention for Young Children (TACSEI): http://www.challengingbehavior.org/

Print Resources

- National Professional Development Center on Inclusion. (2011). *Research synthesis points on practices that support inclusion.* Chapel Hill: University of North Carolina, Frank Porter Graham (FPG) Child Development Institute, Author. Retrieved from http://npdci.fpg.unc.edu/
- Peterson, C.A., Fox, L., & Santos, A. (Eds.). (2009). Quality inclusive services in a diverse society. *Young Exceptional Children, Monograph Series No. 11.* Missoula, MT: Division for Early Childhood.
- Rush, D.R., & Shelden, M.L. (2011). *The early childhood coaching handbook.* Baltimore, MD: Paul H. Brookes Publishing Co.
- Sandall, S.R., & Schwartz, I.S. (2008). *Building blocks for teaching preschoolers with special needs* (2nd ed.). Baltimore, MD: Paul H. Brookes Publishing Co.

HOW SHOULD I USE THIS BOOK?

How you use this book will depend on your role and where you are in the process of implementing inclusion. This guidebook can be used in several ways:

- As an individual resource for administrators, leaders, and aspiring leaders
- As an in-house resource for programs implementing inclusion

- As a leadership resource for leaders building partnerships in the community, district, and/or state
- As an introductory textbook for leadership and teacher preparation programs
- As a leadership tool to reinforce leadership practices across state and local professional development events

Tools to guide your work are embedded in each chapter and can be identified by the following elements separated from the main text:

- Tables
- Figures
- Forms
- Resource corners
- Activity corners
- Quick tips
- FYIs

These elements are designed to encourage reflection, both individually and within groups. Instructors may use these elements to encourage reflection, exploration, and discussion in coursework or in professional development events. Leaders may use these elements to encourage individual practitioner reflection or to facilitate team reflection and activity. Similarly, administrators may find them useful in reviewing both resources and supports in the field and the larger community.

Further enhancing the content are vignettes that illustrate the complexities in facilitating preschool inclusion in program or community settings. The vignettes are unique to the concepts and issues presented in each chapter. Hopefully, future editions of this book will share additional administrator and leader experiences and lessons learned.

REFERENCES

Barnett, W.S., Carolan, M.E., Fitzgerald, J., & Squires, J.H. (2011). *The state of preschool 2011: State preschool yearbook.* New Brunswick, NJ: National Institute for Early Education Research. Retrieved from http://nieer.org/sites/nieer/files/2011yearbook.pdf

Beckman, P.J., Barnwell, D., Horn, E., Hanson, M.J., Gutierrez, S., & Lieber, J. (1998). Communities, families, and inclusion. *Early Childhood Research Quarterly, 13*(1), 125–150.

Bricker, D. (1995). The challenge of inclusion. *Journal of Early Intervention, 19*(3), 179–194. doi:10.1177/105381519501900301

DEC/NAEYC. (2009). *Early childhood inclusion: A joint position statement of the Division for Early Childhood (DEC) and the National Association for the Education of Young Children (NAEYC).* Chapel Hill: University of North Carolina, Frank

Porter Graham (FPG) Child Development Institute. Retrieved from http://www.naeyc.org/positionstatements

Gupta, S.S. (2011, January). *Policy brief: Strategies to facilitate and sustain the inclusion of young children with disabilities.* Denver: University of Colorado Denver, Pyramid Plus: The Colorado Center for Social and Emotional Competence and Inclusion. Retrieved from http://www.pyramidplus.org/policywork/advisory

Hayden, P., Frederick, L., & Smith, B.J. (2003). *A road map for facilitating collaborative teams.* Longmont, CO: Sopris West.

Individuals with Disabilities Education Improvement Act (IDEA) of 2004, PL 108-446, 20 U.S.C. §§ 1400 *et seq.*

Lazara, A., Daneher, J., Kraus, R., Goode, S., Hipps, C., & Festa, C. (2011). *Section 619 Profile* (18th ed.). Chapel Hill: University of North Carolina, Frank Porter Graham (FPG) Child Development Institute, National Early Childhood Technical Assistance Center. Retrieved from http://www.nectac.org/~pdfs/pubs/sec619_2011.pdf

Lieber, J., Beckman, P.J., Hanson, M.J., Janko, S., Marquart, J.M., Horn, E., & Odom, S.L. (1997). The impact of changing roles on relationships between professionals in inclusive programs for young children. *Early Education and Development, 8*(1), 67–82. doi:10.1207/s15566935eed0801_6

National Professional Development Center on Inclusion (NPDCI). (2009). *Research synthesis points on early childhood inclusion.* Chapel Hill: University of North Carolina, Frank Porter Graham (FPG) Child Development Institute, Author. Retrieved from http://npdci.fpg.unc.edu/sites/npdci.fpg.unc.edu/files/resources/NPDCIResearchSynthesisPoints-10-2009_0.pdf

National Professional Development Center on Inclusion. (2011). *Research synthesis points on practices that support inclusion.* Chapel Hill: University of North Carolina, Frank Porter Graham (FPG) Child Development Institute, Author. Retrieved from http://npdci.fpg.unc.edu/

Peterson, C.A., Fox, L., & Santos, A. (Eds.). (2009). Quality inclusive services in a diverse society. *Young Exceptional Children, Monograph #11.* Missoula, MT: Division for Early Childhood.

Rush, D.R., & Shelden, M.L. (2011). *The early childhood coaching handbook.* Baltimore, MD: Paul H. Brookes Publishing Co.

Ryan, S., Whitebook, M., Kipnis, F., & Sakai, L. (2011). Professional development needs of directors leading in a mixed service delivery preschool program. *Early Childhood Research and Practice, 13*(1), 1–15.

Sandall, S., Hemmeter, M.L., Smith, B.J., & McLean, M.E. (2005). *DEC recommended practices: A comprehensive guide for practical application in early intervention/early childhood special education.* Missoula, MT: Sopris West.

Sandall, S.R., & Schwartz, I.S. (2008). *Building blocks for teaching preschoolers with special needs* (2nd ed.). Baltimore, MD: Paul H. Brookes Publishing Co.

Smith, B.J., & Rose, D.J. (1993). *Administrator's policy handbook for preschool mainstreaming: Administrative issues for education series.* Cambridge, MA: Brookline Books.

Smith, B.J., Strain, P., & Ostrosky, M.M. (2004). *Inclusion: The role of the program administrator.* Center on the Social and Emotional Foundations for Early Learning, What Works Brief No. 13. Retrieved from http://csefel.vanderbilt.edu/briefs/wwb13.pdf

Wallace, F., Blase, K., Fixsen, D., & Naoom, S. (2008). *Implementing the findings of research: Bridging the gap between knowledge and practice.* Alexandria, VA: Educational Research Service.

Wolery, R.A., & Odom, S.L. (2000). *An administrator's guide to preschool inclusion.* Chapel Hill: University of North Carolina, Frank Porter Graham (FPG) Child Development Center, Early Childhood Research Institute on Inclusion. Retrieved from http://www.fpg.unc.edu/sites/fpg.unc.edu/files/resources/reports-and-policy-briefs/ECRII_Administrators_Guide_2000.pdf

For Barbara J. Smith, Ph.D.
You inspired us with leadership, humor, and passion.

For Max

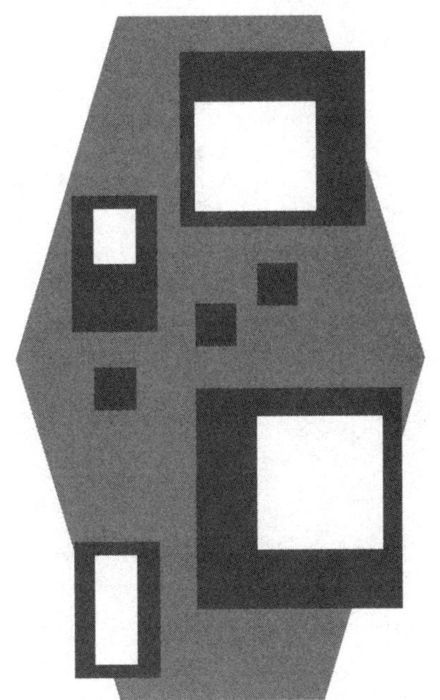

SECTION I

Inclusion, Policy, and Research

CHAPTER 1

What Is Inclusion?

Sarika S. Gupta

Ava is the director of a private preschool program that is operated by a corporation. She is also enrolled in a leadership licensure program in which she is learning about provisions of federal laws that support the inclusion of young children with disabilities. The timing could not be better, because several families in her community have approached her about the prospect of enrolling younger siblings with disabilities into the program within 2–3 years. Ava learns through conversations with her graduate cohort that her program may be given extra funding to support children eligible for preschool special education services. She uses a course assignment to develop a rationale for inclusion that she can present to the administration.

The following week, Ava shares her rationale with the administration, adding that the program would receive additional funding from the state to support inclusion. Driven by the extra funding, the administration encourages Ava to begin including children with disabilities immediately. They anticipate that this immediate change in policy would not only show the state that the program is following federal requirements but also provide the program with much needed funding to support day-to-day operations. Ava, however, feels hesitant. She had hoped the administration would support inclusion, but she sees this initial case presentation as a first step in developing a 2-year plan to learn more about inclusion and staff needs before enrolling children with disabilities. She thinks that much more consideration is needed to implement inclusion successfully. The administration disregards Ava's suggestion for a 2-year plan and moves ahead with developing a policy and recruitment plan. Within 2 weeks, 3 children with disabilities are enrolled in the program, 2 in a classroom of 18. Teachers express frustration at the immediate change, claiming they are ill-equipped to support these new children. When invited to observe, Ava notices that the new children are mostly sitting off to the side, apart from their peers, and uninvolved in daily routines. Though the administration proudly celebrates the new inclusive program with the media and parents in the community, Ava knows this is not what inclusion should look like.

Mr. Oby is 3-year-old Arjun's service coordinator. Arjun was diagnosed with developmental delay just before his 3rd birthday and beginning preschool. His parents suspect that he has an autism spectrum disorder but agree with the developmental delay diagnosis on the condition that he be placed in a classroom with typical peers so he can learn social and communication skills from them.

During Arjun's individualized education program (IEP) meeting, the district preschool special education specialist suggests that Arjun be placed in a public preschool special education program, designated a "preschool autism classroom." Arjun's parents are hesitant about enrolling him in this program, believing he would benefit from being around typically developing peers. They notice that, after he spends time with his typically developing 4-year-old cousin, he is more social and uses language to communicate his needs. They think that with these types of opportunities he would learn more about how to interact with others from same-age peers.

Mr. Oby assures Arjun's parents that, despite the name, the classroom is inclusive in that the majority of children are typically developing; however, rather than rush the decision, Mr. Oby encourages Arjun's parents to visit two additional classrooms Arjun could likely attend. In both schools, Arjun's parents visit two full-day preschool classrooms, each with eight children. Both classrooms are staffed with one lead teacher with a master's degree in early childhood special education (ECSE) and an assistant with a bachelor's degree in education or a related field. The principal of the first school explains that the majority of children in this classroom are typically developing and that children with diagnosed disabilities are included in the classroom. The lead teacher in the classroom of the second school explains the same structure as the first, except that the class has more children with disabilities, four specifically with autism.

After their visits, Arjun's parents debrief with Mr. Oby. Though the arrangements seem the same, they had noticed that the classroom environments seem different. In the first school, they had not been able to determine which children have disabilities. All the children had been engaged in daily routines and with each other, and a variety of visual supports were broadly seen across the classroom. This contrasted with the second classroom in which Arjun's parents had been immediately able to determine which children had disabilities by their pictures around the room. Near the circle area, pictures of the four children with disabilities had been displayed with a series of checks and notepads. Outside of the bathroom, goals for each of these children had also been posted. Halfway through the morning, Arjun's parents also had observed that three of the four children with disabilities leave the classroom. Two had left the classroom with one adult, and the other one had left the classroom with a different adult. Why are the students leaving the program, they wondered? Is not the purpose of an inclusive program to support each child's individual needs in the same setting and within the same activities as their typical peers? Also, why are the children with disabilities' needs highlighted more than their typically developing peers' needs?

Mr. Oby patiently listens to Arjun's parents' questions and concerns. He then chooses his words carefully, beginning with, "Both classrooms are inclusive and here's why."

Collette was born with a visual disability. At the age of 4, she was diagnosed as legally blind, which qualified her for preschool special education services within her local district. Despite her diagnosis and her assessment team's recommendation that she attend a special program for children with a range of visual impairments, her parents think it best that she remain in her current private preschool program that "includes children with special needs." The family hired a nurse who provided morning child care and then took Collette to school for a social "lunch bunch." She then remained at the school each afternoon for her preschool program.

Collette was 1 of 18 in a classroom of 5-year-olds and the only child with a diagnosed disability. The classroom was staffed with two teachers and one assistant. The school also employed in-house specialists, such as an occupational therapist, a physical therapist, a speech-language pathologist, and a school psychologist. Through the local district's eligibility determination process, Collette's assessment team determined that she needed visual, occupational, and physical therapies. The team consisted of Collette's primary teachers, the private school occupational therapist, the district visual specialist, the district psychologist, Collette's parents, and a special education advocate. With the family, the team developed an IEP that outlined 2 hours of visual therapy in the classroom setting, 1 hour of occupational therapy, and 30 minutes of activity-based based physical therapy in her classroom with her peers each week.

Two months later, Collette's mom decided to take a day off to visit Collette in school. She spent the entire day observing Collette. Collette seemed fully engaged in the daily routine, signing in at arrival, making independent choices, eating snacks on her own, offering suggestions during the morning meeting, and interacting with her peers throughout the day. On this particular day, Collette's visual therapist was also visiting. She usually worked with Collette in the classroom, but today she thought Collette should practice some targeted braille reading in a quieter setting, so she pulled Collette out of the classroom for an hour. Mom observed the interaction and thought that it did not seem to meet the 2 hours of visual therapy in the classroom setting that they had outlined in Collette's IEP. Concerned, Mom approached Collette's teachers. The teachers acknowledged Mom's concerns and suggested she speak to Collette's visual therapist, who might be able to provide more insight into why she pulled Collette out of the classroom. Mom believed what she saw was not inclusion . . . but was it?

Ms. Oviya is in her 7th year of teaching preschool at the local temple. This year her director asked her to join the Inclusion Task Force, a small group of select teachers, parents, and leaders charged with creating a vision for inclusion in the temple. Task Force teacher members thought the best way to develop a vision was to survey staff to determine their understanding of inclusion and what might impede inclusive efforts. One teacher Ms. Oviya spoke to suggested that children with disabilities be directed to specific classrooms. When asked why, this teacher explained simply that she did not have the expertise or the time to learn how to include children with disabilities and thought that they would be better served by being placed in a class with a teacher with specialized knowledge of disabilities and individualized instruction. Ms. Oviya considered this teacher's suggestion. She thought the teacher made a valid point: Children are served better when teachers know how to support their individual needs. She wondered, would the practice of directing children into specific classrooms negate the program's vision for inclusion? Also, should only the teachers with specialized experience be expected to include children with disabilities? Or should a teacher's lack of knowledge and experience be justification enough to place children in classrooms in which they would have more potential to develop and learn? If the temple was instituting a programwide vision for inclusion, would each classroom need to be prepared to include children with disabilities?

WHAT IS INCLUSION?

To understand inclusion, one should understand the laws that support it. IDEA (2004) states that

> Each public agency must ensure that—
>
> (i) To the maximum extent appropriate, children with disabilities, including children in public or private institutions or other care facilities, are educated with children who are nondisabled.
>
> (ii) Special classes, separate schooling, or other removal of children with disabilities from the regular educational environment occurs only if the nature or severity of the disability is such that education in regular classes with the use of supplementary aids and services cannot be achieved satisfactorily. (34 C.F.R. §§ 300.114 [a][2][i] and [ii])

Further clarified by Vinh and Henninger in Chapter 2, this provision means that

> in determining the educational placement of a child with a disability, including a *preschool child with a disability*, each public agency must ensure that the child is educated in the school that he or she would attend if nondisabled unless the Individualized Education Program (IEP) of a child with a disability requires another arrangement. (34 C.F.R. § 300.116 [c]; emphasis mine)

In practice, inclusion is best described by the Division of Early Childhood (DEC) and National Association for the Education of Young Children (NAEYC) (2009):

> Early childhood inclusion embodies the values, policies, and practices that support the right of every infant and young child and his or her family, regardless of ability, to participate in a broad range of activities and context as full members of families, communities, and society. The desired results of inclusive experiences for children with and without disabilities and their families include a sense of belonging and membership, positive social relationships and friendships, and development and learning to reach their full potential. (p. 2)

RESOURCE CORNER 1.1

DEC/NAEYC Inclusion Position Statement

Download and read the DEC/NAEYC (2009) joint position statement on early childhood inclusion, available here: http://www.naeyc.org/files/naeyc/file/positions/DEC_NAEYC_EC_updatedKS.pdf

Pause here to review the DEC/NAEYC inclusion position statement, cited in Resource Corner 1.1. As a field and community, we agree that inclusion is a right that values the membership and participation of children with disabilities in typical settings (e.g., Bricker, 1995). We also agree that inclusion involves much more than physically placing a child in a setting with typical peers, as shown in Figure 1.1. Children can simply be *integrated* into a classroom setting but not encouraged to participate in daily routines with peers, as shown in the bottom bubble on the right. Or they may attend the same school as their typically developing peers but be segregated in a separate classroom, away from peers and/or other children with disabilities. Of the greatest concern is when children with disabilities are entirely excluded from the setting, from children, and from adults with which they would generally interact if they did not have a disability. As a philosophy and approach, inclusion is our aim, the starting place, and the beginning expectation for all young children across a continuum of settings available for children.

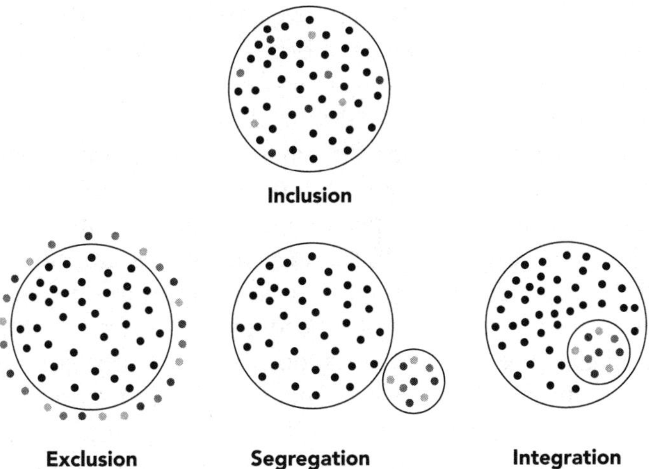

Figure 1.1. Models of inclusion.

Inclusion is a right that values the membership and participation of children with disabilities in typical settings.

Where we struggle is in defining how inclusion looks in practice.

ACTIVITY CORNER 1.1
Review, Reflect, and Discuss

With a partner, review the vignettes and answer the following questions:

- What seem to be the expectations for inclusion?
- Are there conflicting views of inclusion?
- Identify two similar views of inclusion across vignettes.
- Identify two contrasting views of inclusion across vignettes.
- Are they consistent with DEC/NAEYC's definition of inclusion?
- Do they reflect the concept of inclusion as depicted in Figure 1.1?

Our expectations for inclusion are shaped largely by our expectations for children and instruction. For instance, do you believe that all children have the right to learn and that they are capable of learning with appropriate supports? Do you feel some children need additional assistance? Do you possess the knowledge and skill set to support children's individualized needs? Do you share a similar vision as your colleagues for what inclusion should look like in a classroom setting? The answers to these questions are rooted in our cultural upbringing, our personal and educational experiences, and our overall competence in feeling we can (or cannot . . . yet!) successfully support children of varying abilities in one early childhood setting. They are also influenced by the infrastructural supports around us—the program mission, administrator support, opportunities for professional development, and other external factors you will learn more about in what follows. Taking time to reflect on what you personally and culturally believe will be an important first step. Comparing and contrasting your perspective with the established definition for early childhood inclusion is the next one (see Resource Corner 1.1). Take a moment to reflect on what you have learned about inclusion so far by completing Activity Corner 1.1.

We aim in this book to strengthen your understanding of inclusion. We began this chapter by describing what inclusion is and exploring some of the factors that can shape our perception of what inclusion should look like. It is just as important to acknowledge what we know about inclusion.

Researchers at the University of North Carolina at Chapel Hill summarized more than 30 years of research into nine key points (Buysse & Hollingsworth, 2009; National Professional Development Center on Inclusion, 2009, pp. 1–5):

1. Inclusion takes many different forms.
2. Universal access to inclusive programs for children with disabilities is far from a reality.
3. Inclusion can benefit children with and without disabilities.
4. Factors such as child characteristics, policies, resources, and attitudes influence the acceptance and implementation of inclusion.
5. Specialized instruction is an important component of inclusion and a factor affecting child outcomes.
6. Collaboration among parents, teachers, and specialists is a cornerstone of high-quality inclusion.
7. Families of young children with disabilities generally view inclusion favorably, although some express concerns about the quality of early childhood programs and services.
8. The quality of early childhood programs that enroll children with disabilities is as good as, or slightly better than, the quality of programs that do not enroll these children.
9. Early childhood professionals may not be adequately prepared to serve young children with disabilities and their families in inclusive programs.

Perhaps the most challenging point for families, practitioners, and leaders to wrap their heads around is the first: *Inclusion takes many different forms.* We illustrated this in the vignettes. It should come as no surprise that children have differing needs and that their IEPs are likely to reflect these needs (see Chapter 2 to learn more about IEPs). A continuum of early childhood settings allows for this flexibility (Cate, Diefendorf, McCullough, & Peters, 2011):

Settings with Typical Peers/Inclusive Services

- General early childhood program with support in classroom
- Blended program

Setting with Typical Peers/Separate Services

- General EC program pull-out
- Part-time general / part-time special education
- Social inclusion
- Reverse inclusion

Separate Settings

- Separate program
- Separate school

Inclusion takes many different forms.

The key is determining which setting benefits the child the most. We entrust this decision to experienced members of the IEP team, which includes the child's parents. Unfortunately, "inclusive opportunities for young children with disabilities are often not systematic, comprehensive or necessarily of high quality" (NECTAC, 2011, p. 1). Administrators and leaders may leave eligibility determination and placement decisions to IEP teams, but they must lay a foundation for high-quality inclusion (Delaney, 2001). One way for administrators and leaders to do this is to insist on building responsive, high-quality settings that address three key features: access, participation, and supports (DEC/NAEYC, 2009).

The key is determining which setting benefits the child the most.

Access

1. Are a wide range of learning opportunities, activities, settings, and environments accessible to children?
2. Are multiple and varied forms for instruction and learning available to children?

Participation

1. Beyond access, are children provided individualized accommodations and supports to participate fully in play and learning activities with peers and adults?
2. Beyond physically including children in a classroom setting, are adults promoting belonging, participation, and engagement of all children?
3. Beyond physical placement of children in a typical classroom, are adults scaffolding children's learning and participation?
4. Are adults promoting social-emotional development and positive behaviors in all children?
5. Are adults aware of systematic ways (e.g., tiered models) to identify and address the individualized needs of all children?

Supports

1. Beyond access and opportunities for meaningful participation, is there a larger system of supports?
2. Are family members, teachers, specialists, leaders, and administrators each provided opportunities to learn more about inclusion and acquire the skills and dispositions needed to implement and sustain inclusion?
3. Do those implementing inclusion feel supported in their day-to-day work with children with disabilities and the children's families?
4. Is inclusion supported by leaders, administrators, and policies?
5. Are all parties aware of what inclusion means?
6. Are all parties knowledgeable about inclusion, how to provide individualized instruction, and how to address the priorities of children with disabilities and their families?

Insist on building responsive, high-quality settings that address three key features: access, participation, and supports.

When leaders insist on these features, they set the "tone and philosophy" for their programs, modeling positive attitudes and high expectations for inclusion (Smith, Strain, & Ostrosky, 2004, p. 2). In turn, these features ensure that children are not simply placed in a setting with typical peers but are fully and meaningfully engaged with others in these settings.

Welcoming children of all abilities into typical settings both in early childhood programs and beyond in meaningful ways is what inclusion is all about (Odom, Buysse, & Soukakou, 2011). As an administrator and leader, you are in a prime position to systematically build a vision and plan for high-quality inclusion in your program. Such an effort requires "considerable thought and planning" on a personal level but also from conceptual and programmatic standpoints, taking into account varying perspectives of families, your staff, and others who can potentially support or impede such efforts (Bricker, 1995, p. 180).

As an administrator and leader, you are in a prime position to systematically build a vision and plan for high-quality inclusion in your program.

Leading the charge and vision for inclusion is important work. Hopefully you find this book useful in reflecting first on your understanding, beliefs, and practices, then leading and empowering others to do the same. Pause now to apply the information presented in this chapter in Activity Corner 1.2 before proceeding to Chapter 2.

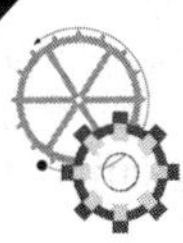

ACTIVITY CORNER 1.2
Review, Reflect, and Apply

Revisit the vignettes and answer the following questions:

- Review the nine key research points on early childhood inclusion. In which vignettes is more information needed? What additional information would be useful?
- Where on the "continuum of early childhood settings" do these vignette examples fall?
- Are you able to determine whether the three key features of high-quality inclusion—access, participation, and supports—are addressed in the vignettes?

(continued)

ACTIVITY CORNER 1.2 (*continued*)
Review, Reflect, and Apply

- Weigh the pros and cons of developing an inclusion policy and including children with disabilities without giving your staff advance notice. Will this effort be successful? Why or why not? What barriers are likely to emerge? How might your staff respond?
- In your experience, what leadership qualities do you perceive to be effective or not effective? Why?
- Take a moment to list your concerns and questions about including young children with disabilities into your program.

REFERENCES

Bricker, D. (1995). The challenge of inclusion. *Journal of Early Intervention, 19*(3), 179–194. doi:10.1177/105381519501900301

Buysse, V., & Hollingsworth, H.L. (2009). Program quality and early childhood inclusion: Recommendations for professional development. *Topics in Early Childhood Special Education, 29,* 119–128. doi:10.1177/0271121409332233

Cate, D., Diefendorf, M., McCullough, K., & Peters, M. (2011). *Considerations for making finance decisions to promote inclusion.* Chapel Hill: University of North Carolina, Frank Porter Graham (FPG) Child Development Institute, National Early Childhood Technical Assistance Center. Retrieved from http://projects.fpg.unc.edu/~pfi/pdfs/think_tank_2_2012/28-Considerations_for_making_finance_decisions_to_promote_inclusion.pdf

DEC/NAEYC. (2009). *Early childhood inclusion: A joint position statement of the Division for Early Childhood (DEC) and the National Association for the Education of Young Children (NAEYC).* Chapel Hill: University of North Carolina, Frank Porter Graham (FPG) Child Development Institute. Retrieved from http://www.naeyc.org/positionstatements

Delaney, E.M. (2001). The administrator's role in making inclusion work. *Young Children, 56*(5), 66–70.

Individuals with Disabilities Education Improvement Act (IDEA) of 2004, PL 108-446, 20 U.S.C. §§ 1400 *et seq.*

Individuals with Disabilities Education Act (IDEA) Regulations, 34 C.F.R. §§ 300 *et seq.*

National Early Childhood Technical Assistance Center (NECTAC). (2011). *Evaluation summary of the Expanding Opportunities Interagency Inclusion Initiative.* Retrieved from http://www.nectac.org/~pdfs/pubs/exp_opps_eval_summary.pdf

National Professional Development Center on Inclusion (NPDCI). (2009). *Research synthesis points on early childhood inclusion.* Chapel Hill: University of North Carolina, Frank Porter Graham (FPG) Child Development Institute, Author. Retrieved from http://npdci.fpg.unc.edu/sites/npdci.fpg.unc.edu/files/resources/NPDCIResearchSynthesisPoints-10-2009_0.pdf

Odom, S.L., Buysse, V., & Soukakou, E. (2011). Inclusion for young children with disabilities: A quarter century of research perspectives. *Journal of Early Intervention, 33,* 344–356. doi:10.1177/1053815111430094

Smith, B.J., Strain, P., & Ostrosky, M.M. (2004). *Inclusion: The role of the program administrator.* Center on the Social and Emotional Foundations for Early Learning, What Works Brief No. 13. Retrieved from http://csefel.vanderbilt.edu/briefs/wwb13.pdf

CHAPTER 2

What Federal Laws and Policies Govern Inclusion?

Megan E. Vinh and William R. Henninger, IV

Administrators and leaders should understand the federal laws and policies that support inclusion. Federal law guides the inclusion of children and youth with disabilities, whereas earlier case law influenced the notion that all children be included in the general education system.

Federal policies, such as Part B of IDEA and Section 504 of the Rehabilitation Act of 1973 (PL 93-112), require that we consider providing services to children with disabilities in typical settings so that children are included with their typically developing peers. Case law helps us understand how to interpret these laws to include children with disabilities. Both federal policies and case laws were influenced by the work of civil rights activists, parent advocates, and early childhood policy makers.

Federal policies and case laws were influenced by the work of civil rights activists, parent advocates, and early childhood policy makers.

This chapter describes the major federal policies and case laws that guide the inclusion of preschoolers with disabilities. It begins with definitions of key terms then provides an overview of preschool special education, or Part B-619, and early intervention, or Part C, in IDEA. Following this is a description of the provisions, or requirements, within IDEA that support the inclusion of young children—namely, *least restrictive environment* in Part B and *natural environment* in Part C. Also addressed are several other key federal policies, such as the ADA, Section 504 of the Rehabilitation Act of 1973, and the Improving Head Start for School Readiness Act of 2007, and how they support inclusion in early learning programs. The chapter concludes with a discussion of the relevance of both laws and policies to the inclusion of preschool-age children.

DEFINITIONS

Free appropriate public education (FAPE)—FAPE means that a child with disabilities will receive special education and related services without charge and under public supervision and direction in an appropriate preschool setting that meets the needs of an individual child as discussed in that child's IEP (34 C.F.R. § 300.17).

Individualized education program (IEP)—The IEP is a written document required by IDEA for all eligible children, ages

3–21, receiving special education services through Part B. The IEP describes a child's current level of functioning and educational plan (e.g., instructional strategies, assessment, and time line). This plan is developed in conjunction with parents and an IEP team (Coleman, 2007).

Individualized family service plan (IFSP)—The IFSP is similar to the IEP in that it is a written individualized plan. It describes supports for children from birth to 3 years old, who are eligible for Part C, and their families. The plan includes not only assessment procedures, the child's current level of development, goals, and time lines but also a description of the family strengths, priorities, and needs. The IFSP is developed collaboratively by the family and an early intervention team (Coleman, 2007).

Office of Special Education Programs (OSEP)—OSEP, in the U.S. Department of Education, oversees implementation of IDEA. In addition, OSEP provides leadership and funding to improve results for children with disabilities, from birth to 21 years old (U.S. Department of Education, Office of Special Education and Rehabilitative Services, 2004). For example, they support state efforts to collect data documenting children's progresses while participating in Part B-Section 619 and Part C services (Edelman, 2011).

Supplementary aids and services—These are aids, services, and other supports that are provided in general education classes, other education-related settings, and extracurricular and nonacademic settings that enable children with disabilities to be educated along with children without disabilities to the maximum extent appropriate (34 C.F.R. § 300.42).

"We conclude that in the field of public education the doctrine of separate but equal has no place. Separate educational facilities are inherently unequal . . . segregation [in public education] is a denial of the equal protection of the laws" (*Brown v. Board of Education*, 1954).

INTRODUCTION

Samuel is a 4-year-old boy with autism that attends a public preschool program with his typically developing peers. He loves to go to school but sometimes has difficulty communicating, which makes it difficult for him to make friends and participate in day-to-day classroom activities. His difficulty communicating has led to challenging behavior within the classroom, such as hitting other children and becoming easily frustrated and irritable. This behavior has become a challenge for his classroom teacher, who is unsure if he has been placed in the correct setting. His parents believe that being included with his typically developing peers will be the most successful way to help Samuel prepare for kindergarten. Samuel has an annual IEP meeting coming up next month, and placement is something that will be discussed with his family, who believe a paraprofessional may need to be provided, and his teacher and other team members, who believe he needs to receive services in a classroom for children with similar needs. This is not an uncommon scenario when discussing the challenges of including children with disabilities in a classroom with their typically developing peers. Parents and teachers may not always be on the same page, so it is important to understand what regulations say or do not say regarding inclusion.

"Early childhood inclusion embodies the values, principles, and practices that support the right of every infant and young child and his or her family, regardless of ability, to participate in a broad range of activities and contexts as full members of families, communities, and society" (DEC/NAEYC, 2009, p. 1). Federal laws, such as IDEA (see FYI 2.1 for more information); the ADA; Section 504 of the Rehabilitation Act of 1973; and the Improving Head Start for School Readiness Act of 2007 recognize and support equal educational opportunities and inclusion of children with disabilities based on the educational, social, and developmental benefits (CONNECT, 2009). Section 1400(5) of IDEA states, "Almost 30 years of research and experience has demonstrated that the education of children with disabilities can be made more effective by . . . ensuring their access to the general education curriculum in the regular classroom, to the maximum extent possible" (CONNECT, 2009, p. 2).

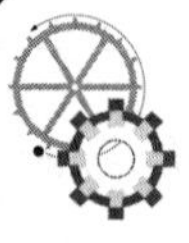

ACTIVITY CORNER 2.1
Individualized Education Program

Have you participated on an IEP team? What have your experiences been with IEP team meetings? What went well? What was challenging?

FYI 2.1

Individuals with Disabilities Education Act at a Glance: Major Provisions

- Zero reject: All children eligible for Part B services, regardless of the severity or type of their disability, are entitled to FAPE.
- Child find: This provision requires that all states have policies and procedures in effect that ensure all children with disabilities who are in need of special education and related services (including children with disabilities who are homeless or wards of the state and children with disabilities attending private schools), regardless of the severity of their disability, are identified, located, and evaluated.
- A child with a disability: This includes any child with an intellectual disability (formerly mental retardation), a hearing impairment (including deafness), a speech or language impairment, a visual impairment (including blindness), a serious emotional disturbance, an orthopedic impairment, autism, a traumatic brain injury, any other health impairment, a specific learning disability, deaf-blindness, or multiple disabilities who needs special education and related services.
- Nondiscriminatory identification and evaluation: All children are entitled to a nondiscriminatory identification and evaluation process that
    - Uses a variety of assessment tools and strategies to gather functional, developmental, and academic information about the child (no single measure or assessment can be used as the sole criterion for determining whether a child has a disability)
    - Uses technically sound instruments
    - Uses assessments and strategies that are selected and administered so as not to be discriminatory on a racial or cultural basis
    - Uses assessments and strategies that can be administered in a child's native language or other mode of communication

(continued)

FYI 2.1 (*continued*)

Individuals with Disabilities Education Act at a Glance: Major Provisions

- o Uses assessments and strategies that are administered by trained and knowledgeable personnel
- IEP for preschool children (as appropriate): This is a written plan for each eligible child with a disability that is developed, reviewed, and revised to include the following information:
  - o A statement of the child's present levels of performance, including how the child's disability affects the child's participation in appropriate activities
  - o A statement of measurable annual goals, including academic and functional goals
  - o A description of how the child's progress toward meeting the annual goals will be measured
  - o A statement of the special education, related services, and supplementary aids and services needed
  - o An explanation for why the child will not participate with his or her typically developing peers
  - o A statement of any appropriate accommodations
- The IEP team (see Activity Corner 2.1 for discussion questions related to the IEP): This group includes the parents of the child, not fewer than one general education teacher of the child (if the child is participating in general education), not fewer than one special education teacher of the child, a representative of a public agency, an individual who can interpret the instructional implications of the evaluation results, and (at the discretion of the parents) other individuals who have knowledge or special expertise regarding the child.
- Parental participation: This means that all parents have the right to be fully informed throughout the process in their native language or other mode of communication, provide consent for all activities that require it, participate

in determining services, assist in development of the IEP, and participate in the annual review of the IEP. Parents are critical partners in the process.

- Procedural safeguards: The procedural safeguards required by IDEA are intended to protect the interests of families and children with special needs as well as the special education and the early intervention systems. Early intervention and special education personnel are obligated to provide families with a copy of the procedural safeguards, to explain the procedural safeguards to families, and to support an active adherence to an understanding of these safeguards for all involved.
- Due process: It is important to remember that educators and families are equal partners in the educational process. The IEP team should work collaboratively to make decisions regarding the best interests of a child with a disability. Sometimes, however, agreement cannot be made. IDEA provides specific procedures for filing due process complaints for families and public agencies when disputes arise around the identification, evaluation, or educational placement of a child with a disability or the provision of FAPE to the child.
- FAPE and least restrictive environments (LRE) are also major provisions of IDEA. They are described in this chapter, as they relate to inclusion.

INDIVIDUALS WITH DISABILITIES EDUCATION IMPROVEMENT ACT OF 2004 AND INCLUSION

The first sentence in IDEA states (see Activity Corner 2.2) that

> disability is a natural part of the human experience and in no way diminishes the right of individuals to participate in or contribute to society. Improving educational results for children with disabilities is an essential element of our national policy of ensuring equality of opportunity, full participation, independent living, and economic self-sufficiency for individuals with disabilities. (20 U.S.C. §§ 1400 *et seq.*)

IDEA establishes the rights of and protections for children with disabilities and their families (34 C.F.R. § 300.1[b]). Part B of IDEA,

ACTIVITY CORNER 2.2
Individuals with Disabilities Education Act Reflection

Take a moment to think about the first sentence in IDEA. What are your initial reactions to this statement? What words resonate with you? How does this statement make you feel?

signed into law in 1975 and reauthorized in 1997 and 2004 (Guernsey & Klare, 2008), ensures that children with disabilities ages 3–21 have access to a "free appropriate public education that emphasizes special education and related services designed to meet their unique needs and [to] prepare them for further education, employment, and independent living" (34 C.F.R. § 300.1). Similarly, Part C of IDEA supports states in "developing and implementing a statewide, comprehensive, coordinated, multidisciplinary, interagency system that provides early intervention services for infants and toddlers with disabilities and their families" (34 C.F.R. § 303.1). Next, we describe some of the major provisions of the law that are relevant to preschool inclusion.

Free Appropriate Public Education

Part B of IDEA ensures that all children with disabilities, including preschool-age children, be provided a FAPE. FAPE is defined in IDEA as "Special education and related services that are provided at public expense, under public supervision and direction, and without charge, including an appropriate **preschool,** elementary school, or secondary school in the State involved" (34 C.F.R. §§ 300.17 [a] and [c]).

Part B of IDEA ensures that all children with disabilities, including preschool-age children, be provided a FAPE.

Least Restrictive Environment

Part B of IDEA requires schools to support inclusion for children with disabilities from ages 3–21 through the LRE (CONNECT, 2009). IDEA states,

Each public agency must ensure that—

(i) To the maximum extent appropriate, children with disabilities, including children in public or private institutions or other care facilities, are educated with children who are nondisabled; and
(ii) Special classes, separate schooling, or other removal of children with disabilities from the regular educational environment occurs only if the nature or severity of the disability is such that education in regular classes with the use of supplementary aids and services cannot be achieved satisfactorily. (34 C.F.R. §§ 300.114 [a][2][i] and [ii])

Part B of IDEA requires schools to support inclusion for children with disabilities from ages 3–21 through the LRE.

Furthermore, IDEA states, "In determining the educational placement of a child with a disability, including a *preschool child with a disability,* each public agency must ensure that" the child is educated in the school that he or she would attend if without disabilities unless the IEP of a child with a disability requires another arrangement (34 C.F.R. § 300.116 [c]; emphasis ours). For example, Samuel's LRE is in the general educational environment with his typically developing peers.

Although the federal statute and regulations show a strong preference for inclusion, these regulations do not expressly mandate that public agencies ensure children with disabilities are educated in classes with their peers without disabilities (34 C.F.R. § 300.114 Comments). This policy is also clearer when applied to placement decisions for school-age children (Rose & Smith, 1993). Rous and Smith (2011) stated, "What is the interpretation of removal . . . from the regular educational environment or regular classes when the school does not provide educational programming to preschoolers without disabilities?" (p. 2). This is a pivotal question you should address when considering LRE preschool placement options for children with disabilities. Please see Activity Corner 2.3 for reflection questions.

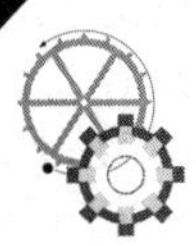

ACTIVITY CORNER 2.3

Least Restrictive Environments

Are children with disabilities included in your program? How might these provisions apply to the inclusion of children with disabilities in your program?

Although the federal statute and regulations show a strong preference for inclusion, these regulations do not expressly mandate that public agencies ensure children with disabilities are educated in classes with their peers without disabilities (34 C.F.R. § 300.114 Comments).

OSEP attempted to address this question in a clarifying comment to the LRE regulations, stating that

> the LRE requirements in 34 CFR §§ 300.114 through 300.118 apply to all children with disabilities, including preschool children who are entitled to FAPE. Public agencies that do not operate programs for preschool children without disabilities are not required to initiate those programs solely to satisfy the LRE requirements of the Act. Public agencies that do not have an inclusive public preschool that can provide all the appropriate services and supports *must explore alternative methods* to ensure that the LRE requirements are met. Examples of such alternative methods might include placement options in private preschool programs or other community-based settings. Paying for the placement of qualified preschool children with disabilities in a private preschool with children without disabilities is one, but not the only, option available to public agencies to meet the LRE requirements. The regulations should allow public agencies to choose an appropriate option to meet the LRE requirements. However, if a public agency determines that placement in a private preschool program is necessary as a means of providing special education and related services to a child with a disability, the program must be at *no cost* to the parent of the child. (34 C.F.R. §§ 300.114–300.118; emphasis ours)

Although these regulations do not mandate inclusion, the support for inclusion is clear. The options laid out in this comment section of IDEA ensure that children are educated in their LRE with a push toward an inclusive environment.

It is also clear that IDEA supports the education of preschool-age children within a classroom of their typically developing peers. OSEP defines a typical early childhood program as "a program that includes a majority (at least fifty percent) of nondisabled children (i.e., children not on IEPs), which includes but is not limited to, Head Start, public or private preschool, public or private Kindergarten, group child development center or child care" (Musgrove, 2012). Please see Activity Corner 2.4 for reflection questions.

Since IDEA's reauthorization in 2004, the number of children with disabilities ages 3–5 attending a typical early childhood

ACTIVITY CORNER 2.4
Inclusion and Your Program

In what early childhood program do you work? Take a moment to reflect on whether your program supports the education of preschool-age children with their typically developing peers. Why or why not?

program at least 10 hours a week has increased. In 2005, 239,082 or 34% of children served under Part B of IDEA attended a typical early childhood program (Data Accountability Center [DAC], 2005). In 2011, 464,720 or 62% of children served under Part B of IDEA attended a typical early childhood program (DAC, 2012). However, only 41% of all children with disabilities ages 3–5 received their special education and related services in a typical early childhood program. This means that most children are enrolled in typical early childhood programs but are not receiving their services within that program.

Most children are enrolled in typical early childhood programs but are not receiving their services within that program.

Natural Environments

Part C of IDEA, also called *early intervention,* supports the inclusion of children birth to 3 years old with the "natural environments" provision. In 34 C.F.R. § 303.26, *natural environments* are defined as "settings that are natural or typical for a same aged infant or toddler without a disability, may include the home or community settings." Furthermore, Part C of IDEA states that early intervention services for infants and toddlers with disabilities are provided "To the maximum extent appropriate, in natural environments; and in settings other than the natural environment that are most appropriate, as determined by the parent and the Individualized Family Service Plan (IFSP) Team, only when early intervention services cannot be achieved satisfactorily in a natural environment" (34 C.F.R. §§ 303.126 [a] and [b]). A natural environment for an infant or toddler may be the child's home, child care, or other location in which the infant or toddler spends most of his or her time.

A natural environment for an infant or toddler may be the child's home, child care, or other location in which the infant or toddler spends most of his or her time.

OTHER RELEVANT POLICIES: AMERICANS WITH DISABILITIES ACT AND SECTION 504 OF THE REHABILITATION ACT OF 1973

The ADA is an antidiscrimination law that protects individuals with disabilities against discrimination in a variety of contexts and settings. Specifically, the ADA bars discrimination against individuals with disabilities in employment situations, state and local government activities, privately operated places of public accommodation (e.g., stores), and communication services (Weber, 2007). Section 504 of the Rehabilitation Act of 1973 states that no "qualified individual with a disability" be subject to discrimination and excluded from or denied access to any program or activity that receives federal financial assistance based on his or her disability (Weber, 2007).

Although more broadly based than IDEA, the ADA and Section 504 safeguard children with disabilities' access to programs and services that are federally funded, and they prohibit discrimination based on service availability, accessibility (e.g., no ramps), and delivery (U.S. Department of Health and Human Services, Office of Civil Rights [OCR] 2006a, 2006b). Under both Section 504 and the ADA, programs cannot deny a child with a disability the opportunity to participate or benefit from a program's services (PEER Project, 1999). Also, a program cannot provide a service that is not as effective as those provided to children without disabilities (PEER Project, 1999). It is important to note that the term *disability* is defined differently than in IDEA. *Section 504 and the ADA define disability more broadly, which may offer protections to children who do not qualify as having a disability under IDEA.* This is important for leaders to know, as the ADA and Section 504 may expand supports to include children with disabilities in publicly supported programs such as Head Start, child care, and state-funded prekindergarten—beyond what IDEA mandates. (Chapter 5 specifically reviews the policies of early childhood programs as they relate to inclusion.)

The ADA and Section 504 safeguard children with disabilities' access to programs and services that are federally funded and prohibit discrimination based on service availability, accessibility (e.g., no ramps), and delivery (U.S. Department of Health and Human Services, 2006).

Improving Head Start for School Readiness Act of 2007 (Head Start Act)

Head Start is a federal program that promotes school readiness for young children in low-income families by providing educational and other services (http://www.acf.hhs.gov/programs/ohs/about/head-start). The Head Start Act was reauthorized in 2007 as Public Law 110-134, "Improving Head Start for School Readiness Act of 2007," to promote school readiness among low-income children by enhancing their cognitive, social, and emotional development (42 U.S.C. §§ 9801 *et seq.*). The act also supports the inclusion of children with special needs in Head Start programs. Specifically, 45 C.F.R. § 1308.5 of the act describes the required recruitment and enrollment of children with disabilities: At least 10% of children enrolled in each Head Start program should be children with disabilities "who are determined to be eligible for special education and related services, or early intervention services under IDEA" (42 U.S.C. § 9837, Section 640 [d][1]).

At least 10% of children enrolled in each Head Start program should be children with disabilities.

Furthermore, Head Start programs are required to partake in outreach and recruitment activities to actively locate and recruit children with disabilities (45 C.F.R. § 1308.5 [a]). Programs cannot deny placement of children based on their disability or its severity "when a parent wishes to enroll the child, the child meets the Head Start age and income eligibility criteria, and Head Start is an appropriate placement according to the child's IEP" (45 C.F.R. § 1308.5 [c]). Similarly,

> staff attitudes and/or apprehensions, inaccessibility of facilities, a child's need to access additional resources, staff's unfamiliarity with a disabling condition or special equipment, and need for personalized special services such as feeding, suctioning, and assistance with toileting, including catheterization, diapering, and toilet training, cannot prohibit a child with disabilities from being served in a Head Start classroom. (45 C.F.R. § 1308.5 [d])

Programs cannot deny placement of children based on their disability or its severity.

Summary

These laws are vitally important in guiding the delivery of inclusive services to children; however, they are often written broadly. In fact, there are instances in which judges in different U.S. district courts rule differently on a case with seemingly similar facts. It is important for program leaders to understand the decisions and the decision-making paradigms used by their U.S. district court when hearing cases that involve LRE. The graph on the following web site can help you understand the geographic boundaries of the U.S. district courts: http://www.uscourts.gov/uscourts/images/CircuitMap.pdf.

It is important for program leaders to understand the decisions and the decision-making paradigms used by their U.S. district court when hearing cases that involve LRE.

Involved parties, such as parents, school districts, and other programs, have the opportunity to appeal decisions made by the U.S. district court. Depending on the decisions, the case can be further appealed until it reaches the highest court in the nation, the U.S. Supreme Court. The rulings made by the Supreme Court set precedence for how the law is to be interpreted. As a result, it is imperative to understand how previous court cases have influenced interpretation of the law on inclusive practices. The following section discusses examples of landmark case law (i.e., Supreme Court cases) that have shaped how we interpret inclusion policy.

CASE LAW

In 1954, *Brown v. the Board of Education* invalidated in a unanimous Supreme Court vote the "separate but equal" doctrine stating that it violated the 14th Amendment, meaning the equal protection for U.S. citizens (Smith & Kozleski, 2005). In this critical case, in which separate schools for African American and Caucasian children were deemed unacceptable, the court stated, "We conclude that in the field of public education, the doctrine of separate but equal has no place. Separate educational facilities are inherently unequal" (Brown v. Board, 1954). Though there was a 20-year delay from the Civil Rights Movement until progress toward equal treatment for children with disabilities was seen, two court cases (i.e., *Pennsylvania Association for Retarded Children* [PARC] *v. Commonwealth of Pennsylvania* [1971] and *Mills v. Board of Education of District of Columbia* [1972]) created a pathway for equal educational access for children with disabilities by establishing that children with disabilities have a right to a public education in an environment in which their typically developing peers would be educated (Chinn, 2004). These cases set the stage for the current system used to educate children with disabilities, specifically preschool-age children with disabilities.

When we talk about case law around inclusion, we are often discussing decisions around LRE. The case law is often complex, with U.S. district courts ruling differently on inclusion cases based on the individual circumstances of each case. There is no hard and fast rule about when and how to include children with disabilities, as it is an individualized decision that the IEP team should make based on the child's best interests. There is, however, a presumption that children will be included with their typically developing peers to the greatest extent appropriate. There is also the presumption that this decision will be made based on a collaborative decision made by the IEP team, including the parents (for more information on collaboration, see Chapter 6). It is important for IEP teams to consider the need for supplemental aids and services to be provided in the LRE for children with disabilities (Weber, 2007). Specifically, when making decisions about placement and provision of services in the LRE, IEP teams should consider whether a child with a disability should receive services in a less restrictive setting with the help of supplemental aids and services.

It is important for IEP teams to consider the need for supplemental aids and services to be provided in the LRE for children with disabilities.

CONCLUDING THOUGHTS

It is critical that administrators and leaders make efforts to include children with their typically developing peers in early childhood programs. To do this, administrators must be aware of the latest laws that govern inclusion. The laws described in this chapter should help you understand the federal requirements that support the inclusion of children with disabilities in your early childhood program. As you will learn in Chapter 3, both children with disabilities and children without disabilities benefit from inclusion. You will also learn in Chapter 5 that, beyond the laws described here, your early learning program may have specific policies that support inclusion.

There are limited publicly supported preschool programs (e.g., Head Start, state-funded prekindergarten) available to eligible young children and their families (Barnett, Carolan, Fitzgerald, & Squires, 2012; Rous & Smith, 2011). As a result, children needing early childhood services are most likely receiving them in a combination of publicly and privately funded settings (Rous & Smith, 2011). For example, a "four-year-old of a single working parent may spend the early morning with family or friend who drops them off at a Head Start center for the morning. The child is transported to the public preschool program in the afternoon, then to a child care program until the parents gets off work" (Rous & Smith, 2011, p. 9). Though potentially challenging for the family to coordinate, this child has the opportunity to be educated and integrated meaningfully into daily routines with his or her peers to make gains that he or she otherwise may not. Very few states provide universal preschool services for children under the age of 4 (Barnett, Carolan, Fitzgerald, & Squires, 2012). Further, 2011–2012 saw "no increase in the percentage of children served in state preK," further challenging the ability of children with disabilities to be served in settings with their typical peers (Barnett, Carolan, Fitzgerald, & Squires, 2012, p. 5). As this chapter illustrates, the regulations that govern inclusion relate to publicly funded settings and opportunities for young children with disabilities. Despite these limitations, administrators and leaders have an important opportunity to model inclusion as a human right for each child that benefits all. Stated best by Judge Becker, "Inclusion is a right, not a privilege for a select few" (*Oberti v. Board of Education*, 1993).

Children needing early childhood services are most likely receiving them in a combination of publicly and privately funded settings.

Very few states provide universal preschool services for children under the age of 4.

REFERENCES

Americans with Disabilities Act (ADA) of 1990, PL 101-336, 42 U.S.C. §§ 12101 *et seq.*

Barnett, W.S., Carolan, M.E., Fitzgerald, J., & Squires, J.H. (2012). *The state of preschool 2012: State preschool yearbook.* New Brunswick, NJ: National Institute for Early Education Research, Rutgers University. Retrieved from http://nieer.org/sites/nieer/files/yearbook2012.pdf

Brown v. Board of Education, 347 U.S. 483 (1954).

Chinn, P.C. (2004). Brown's far reaching impact. *Multicultural Perspectives, 64,* 9–11.

Coleman, J.G. (2007). *The early intervention dictionary: A multi-disciplinary guide to terminology.* Bethesda, MD: Woodbine House.

CONNECT: The Center to Mobilize Early Childhood Knowledge. (2009). *Policy advisory: The law on inclusive education.* Chapel Hill: University of North Carolina, Frank Porter Graham (FPG) Child Development Institute.

Data Accountability Center (DAC). (2005). *Table 1–2: Children ages 3 through 5 served under IDEA, Part B, by disability category and state: Fall 2005.* Retrieved from https://www.ideadata.org/arc_toc7.asp#partbLRE

Data Accountability Center (DAC). (2012). *Table B3–1: Number and percentage of children ages 3 through 5 served under IDEA, Part B, by educational environment and state: Fall 2011.* Retrieved from https://www.ideadata.org/arc_toc13.asp#partbLRE

DEC/NAEYC. (2009). *Early childhood inclusion: A joint position statement of the Division for Early Childhood (DEC) and the National Association for the Education of Young Children (NAEYC).* Chapel Hill: University of North Carolina, Frank Porter Graham (FPG) Child Development Institute. Retrieved from http://www.naeyc.org/positionstatements

Edelman, L. (Producer). (2011). *Child outcomes step by step* (Motion picture). United States: Results Matter, Colorado Department of Education; Desired Results *access* Project, Napa County Office of Education; and Early Childhood Outcomes Center. Retrieved from http://projects.fpg.unc.edu/~eco/pages/videos.cfm

Guernsey, T.F., & Klare, K. (2008). *Special education law* (3rd ed.). Durham, NC: Carolina Academic Press.

Improving Head Start for School Readiness Act of 2007, PL 110-134, 42 U.S.C. §§ 9801 *et seq.*

Individuals with Disabilities Education Act (IDEA) Regulations, 34 C.F.R. §§ 300 *et seq.*

Individuals with Disabilities Education Improvement Act (IDEA) of 2004, PL 108-446, 20 U.S.C. §§ 1400 *et seq.*

Mills v. Board of Education of the District of Columbia. 348 F. Supp. 886 (D. D.C. 1972).

Musgrove, M. (2012, February 29). Dear colleague: Preschool LRE. *OSEP Memos, Dear Colleague Letters and Policy Letters.* Retrieved from http://www2.ed.gov/policy/speced/guid/idea/memosdcltrs/preschoollre22912.pdf

Oberti v. Board of Education, 995 F.2d 1204 (1993).

PEER Project. (1999). *Section 504, the Americans with Disabilities Act, and education reform.* Retrieved from http://www.wrightslaw.com/info/section504_idea.htm

Pennsylvania Association for Retarded Citizens (PARC) v. Commonwealth of Pennsylvania. 334 F. Supp. 1257 (E.D. Pa. 1971).

Rehabilitation Act of 1973, PL 93-112, Section 504, 34 C.F.R. §§ 104 *et seq.*

Rose, D.F., & Smith, B.J. (1993). Preschool mainstreaming: Attitude barriers and strategies for addressing them. *Young Children, 48*(4), 59–62. Reprinted in Paciorek, K.M., & Munro, J.H. (Eds.). (1994, 1995). *Early childhood education: Annual editions.* Guilford, CT: Dushkin Publishing Group.

Rous, B., & Smith, B. (2011). Key national and state policy implementation issues. In C.J. Groark (Series Ed.) & S. Eidelman (Vol. Ed.), *Early childhood intervention: Shaping the future for children with special needs and their families, three volumes: Vol. 1.* Santa Barbara, CA: ABC-CLIO, Praeger.

Smith, A., & Kozleski, E.B. (2005). Witnessing Brown: Pursuit of an equity agenda in American education. *Remedial and Special Education, 26,* 270–280. doi:10.1177/07419325050260050201

U.S. Department of Education, Office of Special Education and Rehabilitative Services. (2004). *Office of Special Education Programs (OSEP) mission statement.* Retrieved from http://www2.ed.gov/about/offices/list/osers/osep/mission.html

U.S. Department of Health and Human Services, Office of Civil Rights (OCR). (2006a, June). *Your rights under Section 504 of the Rehabilitation Act* [factsheet]. Retrieved from http://www.hhs.gov/ocr/civilrights/resources/factsheets

U.S. Department of Health and Human Services, Office of Civil Rights (OCR). (2006b, June). *Your rights under the Americans with Disabilities Act* [factsheet]. Retrieved from http://www.hhs.gov/ocr/civilrights/resources/factsheets

Weber, M.C. (2007). *Understanding disability law.* Newark, NJ: LexisNexis Group.

CHAPTER 3

How Do Children Benefit from Inclusion?

William R. Henninger, IV, and Sarika S. Gupta

Dr. Sloane is a director of a university child development center. The school primarily enrolls preschool-age children of university faculty and staff and occasionally children of families in the community. Currently, the center does not include children with disabilities; however, many of the staff have expressed an interest in doing so for several reasons. Supportive staff members think inclusion is a natural extension of an early childhood philosophy that embraces diversity and celebrates individual differences. They also think that, as the university center, they should be modeling the very practices their field supports. The remainder of the staff have expressed apprehension, however, as they think they do not possess the developmental knowledge or practical experience needed to work with children with more severe disabilities. Their apprehension also stems from wanting to ensure that children make positive gains as a result of participating in their program. Surely the preschoolers with disabilities will benefit from seeing typically developing models, they suggest, but what about the children without disabilities? Will the program still be challenging enough to support their developmental and learning needs? Will these children still make the same gains?

Dr. Sloane admittedly does not have the special education expertise or knowledge of research to reassure staff but believes strongly that all children can benefit from their ability-diverse peers. He considers how best to move forward, seeking the assistance of university faculty in the special education and early childhood programs. Together they point Dr. Sloane toward several research-based resources, articles, and conference presentations that suggest all young children benefit from inclusion.

After reading the first two chapters, it is most likely obvious to you that the early childhood community supports inclusion, as does the law. The next question is why? This chapter turns to research to share how preschoolers both with and without disabilities benefit from participating in high-quality inclusive environments. Researchers have learned a great deal about early childhood inclusion over the past 30 years. Recall from Chapter 1 the research synthesis points developed by Buysse and Hollingsworth (2009) and the National Professional Development Center on Inclusion (NPDCI; 2009). Reviewing the research supporting each point is beyond the scope of this chapter. Instead, here we hone in on the strong evidence supporting children's progress to help readers make a strong case for inclusion in their programs. We know as early childhood educators and leaders that children in early childhood settings are in the midst of immense growth, acquiring knowledge, skills, and abilities in several interconnected realms: social, emotional, physical (e.g., gross motor, fine motor), self-help or adaptive (e.g., dressing independently), communication, and language. Knowing that there is a vast body of research that supports inclusion, we chose to organize this chapter into the short- and long-term benefits, drawing from not only the early childhood inclusion research base but also the wealth of research supporting K–12 inclusion. Research shows that high-quality inclusion can help young children make gains that are not only visible during preschool but also realized much later in life. Further supporting these outcomes are parent and practitioners' perceptions of how exposure to inclusion from an early age can positively influence all children's behaviors and skills (see NPDCI, 2009, Research Synthesis Point #4; see also Chapter 1). After reading this chapter, you will be able to share with families, staff, and professional development providers the ways in which inclusion supports children with and without disabilities' life trajectories, during preschool and into adolescence and adulthood.

Children in early childhood settings are in the midst of immense growth, acquiring knowledge, skills, and abilities in several interconnected realms.

ARE CHILDREN WITH DISABILITIES BEING INCLUDED IN TYPICAL EARLY CHILDHOOD SETTINGS?

Yes, children with disabilities are being included—but much more work is needed. Data from OSEP suggest that the number of preschoolers with disabilities served by Part B of IDEA continues to increase. In 1997, Part B served 565,004 children ages 3–5. By the end of 2006, states collectively reported serving 706,635 children, or 25% more eligible 3- to 5-year olds! Two-fifths, or 44.5%, of these children were served *"in the regular early childhood program*[1]

[1] A "regular early childhood program includes at least 50 percent children without disabilities. Regular early childhood programs include, but are not limited to, Head Start, kindergarten, reverse mainstream classrooms, private preschools, preschool classes offered to an eligible pre-kindergarten population by the public school system and group child care" (U.S. Department of Education, 2011, p. 31).

at least 80% of the time[2] and almost one-fourth (24.2%) of children were served in a *separate class*" (U.S. Department of Education, 2011, p. 32; emphasis ours), suggesting that programs have a long way to go in fully including young children with disabilities.

Programs have a long way to go in fully including young children with disabilities.

One of the more commonly known challenges of inclusion is the lack of high-quality preschool programs (Barnett & Hustedt, 2011). As early childhood educators, we aim to help preschoolers develop and acquire the skills they need to be successful in school as well as later in life, and we do this through thoughtfully designed environments and intentional, structured interactions that scaffold children's growth and learning (e.g., Epstein, 2008; Sandall & Schwartz, 2008). Much of the recent push in early childhood has been toward preparing young children academically for school; however, children must achieve several fundamental social-emotional milestones to effectively apply their knowledge in a kindergarten classroom. To this end, national technical assistance and research centers have been focusing on collecting and disseminating research around the importance of social-emotional development in children's early and lifelong success (e.g., the Center for Social Emotional Foundations of Early Learning; the Technical Assistance Center on Social Emotional Interventions; the National Center on Cultural and Linguistic Responsiveness; the National Center on Parent, Family, and Community Engagement). At the time of this writing, however, National Institute for Early Education Research (NIEER) researchers reported a $715 per student cut in state-funded prekindergarten, or a 15% decrease in state preschool program funding, over the last decade (Barnett et al., 2011, p. 12; NIEER, 2012). These cuts come despite evidence that strong social and emotional beginnings reduce the achievement gap by the time children begin kindergarten and can lead to academic success and future employment (Barnett & Hustedt, 2011). In the nationwide battle for universal high-quality preschool, the inclusion of children with disabilities remains a small but mighty movement that accrues benefits to our nation's children and to our society. We

[2] "Percentage of time spent in the regular early childhood program is defined as the number of hours a child spends per week in the regular early childhood program, divided by the total number of hours the child spends per week in the regular early childhood program plus any hours the child spends per week receiving special education and related services outside of the regular early childhood program, multiplied by 100" (p. 31).

hope you use the evidence presented next to become a champion for young children, particularly preschoolers with disabilities.

Children must achieve several fundamental social-emotional milestones to effectively apply their knowledge in a kindergarten classroom.

CHILDREN WITH DISABILITIES BENEFIT FROM INCLUSION

ECSE and early intervention fields, with support from early childhood leaders, achieved consensus around three general areas that transcend the developmental domains in which young children with disabilities should demonstrate progress toward becoming more meaningfully engaged in their day-to-day lives and across settings. For children with disabilities to be fully integrated into and successful in school and life, they need opportunities to do the following:

- Develop positive social-emotional skills (including social relationships)
- Acquire and use knowledge and skills (including early language/communication and early literacy skills)
- Use appropriate behaviors to meet their own needs (e.g., adaptive or self-help skills such as feeding oneself; see Early Childhood Outcomes Center [n.d.-a])

The rationale for these "functional outcome" areas is that children should be acquiring the rudimentary knowledge, skills, and behaviors needed to develop social competence, think critically, and problem-solve, as well as gain independence in their everyday lives (see Early Childhood Outcomes Center [n.d.-b]). In fact, OSEP uses children's progress data in these outcome categories to measure the success of Part B-619 and Part C services nationwide!

The inclusion of children with disabilities remains a small but mighty movement that accrues benefits to our nation's children and to our society.

Short-Term Benefits

To many, it may appear that typically developing children acquire these functional skills in an effortless manner (Bailey, McWilliams, Buysse, & Wesley, 1998). Research suggests, however, that children who have multiple interactions with peers and adults throughout early childhood show a marked improvement across multiple areas of development (Buysse, Goldman, & Skinner, 2003; Goldstein, 1993; Hart & Risley, 1995). From this information alone, it seems vitally important for children to be placed in situations in which they can interact with peers and adults alike.

The good news is that children with disabilities who are included in high-quality classrooms with their typically developing peers stand to reap positive gains across developmental domains (Holahan & Costenbader, 2000; Odom, 2000; Rafferty, Boettcher, & Griffin, 2001) and likely in the functional outcome areas mentioned earlier, as many parents and practitioners have noted (Rafferty & Griffin, 2005).

Children with disabilities who are included in high-quality classrooms with their typically developing peers stand to reap positive gains across developmental domains.

There is a multitude of research that has been accumulated over 3 decades showing that, when children with disabilities are included in general education settings, they are more likely to exhibit positive social and emotional behaviors at a level that is much greater than their peers who are relegated to programs that serve only children with disabilities (Holahan & Costenbader, 2000; Strain, Bovey, Wilson, & Roybal, 2009). The prevailing theory for this gap is that children in inclusive settings have a chance to interact with peers who demonstrate a broad spectrum of social-emotional abilities (Lamorey & Bricker, 1992; Odom et al., 2002), providing models from whom children with disabilities can learn appropriate social and emotional behaviors (Guralnick, 2001; Odom et al., 2002).

It seems equally important, then, that children with disabilities are given opportunities to interact with higher functioning peers (Goldstein, 1993; Wiener & Tardiff, 2004). Researchers have found that children with disabilities who interact with peers with higher-level social skills often imitate these behaviors and skills in the future (Banda, Hart, & Liu-Gitz, 2010; Holahan & Costenbader, 2000). Researchers Odom and Bailey (2001) cite a body of research that has shown that "children with developmental delays and hearing impairments engage in more advanced forms of play than occurs when participating in play with other children with disabilities" (p. 263). According to a review conducted by Antia and Levine (2001), children who are deaf or hard of hearing are more likely to engage in more advanced levels of play when included with typically developing peers. In addition, when typically developing children are taught strategies to communicate with their hearing-impaired classmates, the quality and quantity of social interactions between them are likely to increase. A similar phenomenon is also noted for children with specific language impairments (Paul-Brown & Caperton, 2001). Finally, young children with autism—a disability characterized by repetitive behaviors and delays in social and communication skills—are more likely to *generalize,* or apply their social skills to new interactions, while in inclusive settings (Strain, 1983), particularly with peer support (Strain et al., 2009).

Researchers have found that children with disabilities who interact with peers with higher-level social skills often imitate these behaviors and skills in the future (Banda, Hart, & Liu-Gitz, 2010; Holahan & Costenbader, 2000).

A recent and rigorous study of the inclusion-driven Learning Experiences and Alternative Program (LEAP) further confirmed improved outcomes in young children with autism in only 2 years (Strain & Bovey, 2011). LEAP is a multifaceted program that integrates research-based practices to support the inclusion of young children with autism in typical preschool classrooms. Researchers trained school personnel over 23 days and provided coaching over a 2-year time frame to ensure staff systematically maintained a high-quality preschool environment, taught typical peers to support social and communication skills (e.g., peer-mediated instruction and intervention), used effective instructional strategies (e.g., errorless teaching, incidental teaching), monitored child progress, and led family skills training (for a thorough description, please see

Strain & Bovey, 2011). Researchers found that children with autism included in LEAP classrooms demonstrated less severity in autistic behaviors than children with autism who were not included in the LEAP program model (Strain & Bovey, 2011). More compelling, perhaps, is that children with autism maintain improved behaviors following program participation as they move into general education classrooms (Strain & Bovey, 2011).

Alternately, when children with disabilities are separated from their peers and excluded from the early childhood classroom, they are unable to observe appropriate social behaviors and are therefore less likely to achieve the fundamental social milestones (Bailey et al., 1998; Holahan & Costenbader, 2000; Peters, 2004) that are linked to later success in school and life. The bottom line is that "regular, sustained interaction" in inclusive classrooms offers children with disabilities opportunities to observe, develop, expand, and generalize their social skills (Strain, McGee, & Kohler, 2001, p. 357).

Although much of the inclusion research has focused on improving children with disabilities' social skills, some emerging evidence also suggests that inclusion, when implemented with fidelity (meaning as designed) and in a high-quality early childhood setting, supports children's cognitive growth greater than situations in which children are not included in a typical early childhood setting (Hoyson, Jamieson, & Strain, 1985; Peters, 2004; Strain & Bovey, 2011; Strain & Hoyson, 2000). In the LEAP preschool program mentioned earlier—a program that includes a blend of necessary supports for children (e.g., classroom and curricular adaptations and modifications), evidence-based instructional approaches (e.g., peer-mediated interventions, positive behaviors supports), dynamic learning objectives, and family skills training to reinforce positive behaviors, all within a routinized schedule—children with social and communication delays across sites show "marked developmental progress on intellectual and language measures" in comparison to their counterparts segregated from typically developing peers (Strain & Bovey, 2011, p. 134). Another study found that preschoolers included in the general education classroom made greater gains around social-emotional development than children with disabilities who were not included (Holahan & Costenbader, 2000). In a paired samples study, children with varying disabilities ages 3–5 were matched on several characteristics (e.g., chronological age, gender, services received, time in program, level of functioning). One child in each pair attended an inclusive classroom, while the other attended a self-contained classroom. Children in the inclusive classroom showed increased social-emotional development compared with their matched pair, as measured by the Brigance Diagnostic Inventory of Early Development (1991).

Clearly, the programs described here are different and target children with varying disabilities; however, all offer what noninclusive programs do not: *the ongoing opportunity to interact with peers of varying academic levels.* Inclusive classrooms are ripe with opportunities to engage children with disabilities in the daily routine and in activities that elicit and challenge academic performance. Typically developing peers, when coached by teachers, can become natural scaffolders of learning and interaction, for example, and evidence to support these types of peer-mediated interventions in the preschool population continues to grow (National Professional Development Center on Autism Spectrum Disorders, 2010). Moreover, the expectations for child growth and development in typical early childhood classrooms are often much greater than expectations for children in segregated classrooms (Guralnick, 1990). Children may be expected to put on their coats themselves, for example, or to manipulate their fingers to pick up and eat a snack. Whatever the expectations may be, they exist for all children. Though they may be accomplished with the right combination of "supplementary aids and services" (see Chapter 2), these higher expectations ultimately lead children with disabilities to achieve more, gain confidence and independence, and develop a stronger sense of self, in their preschool settings and much later in life.

Inclusive classrooms are ripe with opportunities to engage children with disabilities in the daily routine and in activities that elicit and challenge academic performance.

Long-Term Benefits

The long-term benefits of inclusion for children with disabilities continue to emerge. Given the somewhat recent push for inclusion, researchers have not had ample time, resources, or funding to monitor children's progress as they move from inclusive preschool classrooms and into the K–12 and employment arenas. Despite this limitation, "researchers have found that the quality and quantity of young children's social communicative behaviors are highly predictive of long-term developmental and functional outcomes" (U.S. Department of Education, 2011, p. 182). It is from this smaller body of evidence, largely pulled from the K–12 area, that we describe how children benefit from inclusion beyond preschool.

Higher expectations ultimately lead children with disabilities to achieve more, gain confidence and independence, and develop a stronger sense of self.

One area in which children with disabilities who are included in the general education classroom show long-term benefits is in their social-emotional development. Many of the positive social benefits that young children experience in inclusive classrooms continue to be seen when those children are included in K–12 general education classrooms (DeSimone & Parmar, 2006). Students who were included at a younger age and continue to be included with typically developing peers as they become older are likely to demonstrate the following:

- An understanding of socially acceptable behaviors and interactions beyond children educated in segregated classrooms (Cawley, Hayden, Cade, & Baker-Kroczynski, 2002)
- Increased social interactions with peers with and without disabilities (DeSimone & Parmar, 2006; Hughes, Carter, Hughes, Bradford, & Copeland, 2002)
- Fewer feelings of stigmatization associated with pull-out services (Eisenman & Tascione, 2002)

Positive social benefits that young children experience in inclusive classrooms continue to be seen when children with disabilities are included in K–12 general education classrooms.

The research also shows that included children demonstrate academic gains (Brigham, Morocco, Clay & Zigmond, 2006; Idol, 2006), including

- Higher achievement test scores (Wilson & Michaels, 2006)
- High school graduation (Cawley et al., 2002)

It is important to note that some of these findings utilized a mix of children, some of whom were included from an early age and others included closer to their entry into secondary school. However, it seems evident from this research that inclusion has long and meaningful impacts on youngsters with disabilities. There are likely additional benefits that will be brought to light as more data are made available from inclusive settings.

Inclusion has long and meaningful impacts on youngsters with disabilities.

Differing Educational Experiences and the Importance of Early Inclusion In thinking about the ways in which an inclusive classroom differs from a self-contained or general education classroom, many individuals may focus on how instruction is delivered. This detail is important, especially considering the social context of the delivery. Next are two vignettes of children who experience vastly different social experiences in their educational settings, determining the tone for their lifelong learning.

Meet Ziya. Ziya is a 5-year-old boy that began his educational experience in an independent inclusive preschool. Professionals informed his parents that he demonstrated skills consistent with a disability that may affect his motor development, speech development, and some social interaction. Fortunately, in his preschool classroom, Ziya is encouraged at an early age to interact with peers of varying intellectual and social abilities, including children with abilities similar to his as well as children with much stronger social skills. In addition, his well-trained teachers take time to utilize effective instructional techniques to promote his self-regulation skills and appropriate social behaviors, including social stories and prompting. They also facilitate play opportunities with typical peers and teach peers how to encourage Ziya's social skills. As a result, every day that Ziya comes to preschool, he is given multiple opportunities to practice and improve his social interactions. Like a young scientist, he learns on his own what does and does not work through observation, trial and error, and teacher instruction. He is further supported by teachers and peers who reinforce his use of appropriate social behaviors. As Ziya prepares to transition to kindergarten, his parents reflect on how frustrated he was before beginning preschool, unable to express himself and initiate play with his peers. They feel confident that he is now equipped with a rich tapestry of social experiences to draw from as he interacts with older children in his school. His parents largely attribute his abilities to being included with peers who modeled appropriate social behaviors for him.

Meet 5-year-old Azra. Like Ziya, Azra's disability has an impact on her motor, speech, and social skills. Unlike Ziya, her parents were not able to find a public inclusive preschool, so she began her educational experience in her neighborhood child care program. Her providers certainly care for her, but as a result of her disability and her individual support needs, her parents observe her primarily interacting with one child care provider instead of the other children. Her provider, unfortunately, does not have the knowledge base or training to facilitate social interaction and deliver high-quality instruction as Ziya's teachers successfully do. As a result, Azra is not given the same opportunities as Ziya to practice her social skills.

The following year, Azra makes the transition to the same kindergarten as Ziya. The parents of the two are friends and decide to observe Ziya and Azra together during their first week of school. The differences are stark. The parents observe Ziya sitting and engaging in circle time activities, focusing on academic tasks, and easily interacting and playing with peers throughout the day. Azra, in contrast, seems unsure about the routine, and although she can sit with her peers, she seems unsure about how to initiate a conversation, ask questions, or begin collaborative play. Instead, she observes her peers as they play with one another.

The following year in elementary school, Ziya begins to learn key foundational math and literacy concepts. Although he occasionally has trouble understanding specific concepts because of his disability, he is able to rely on his social skills to seek help appropriately and to use suitable social behaviors to develop friendships. Azra seems frustrated, however. Included with her typical peers, she is also learning the same foundational concepts but experiences difficulties understanding concepts due to her disability. These difficulties are evident in her unsuccessful attempts to seek assistance from her peers and teachers. She finds it hard to ask for help appropriately. Out of frustration, she uses inappropriate strategies like grabbing and yelling to seek assistance, but this seems to aggravate her peers and teachers, who see her as "challenging." For this reason, she is unable to make and keep friends. By the time Azra moves into middle school (and eventually high school)—a period in life during which peer groups are of utmost importance—she will likely fall several grade levels behind her peers. Ziya, in the meantime, continues to build friendships. As he moves to middle school and high school, he will likely keep pace with and rely on his peer networks to learn appropriate social behaviors.

Although many early childhood programs may be directed by qualified individuals who can create developmentally appropriate settings, the setting alone is not enough. Physical placement in a high-quality setting alone only offers children with disabilities *access to their peers*. Creating an environment and culture that bolsters meaningful *participation* through daily social interaction, work, and play with appropriate *supports* (e.g., evidence-based instructional strategies, social supports) is also needed for children to make and sustain gains (see Chapter 1). Children with disabilities such as Ziya, who are included early with typical peers and explicitly taught how to interact appropriately with others through evidence-based strategies (e.g., the LEAP program model), experience improved social skills that serve as a foundation for lifelong learning and success. When you start early and "show" young children what is expected of them socially and emotionally using peer models, children are less likely to experience frustration and isolation and more likely to be accepted by others and to excel academically.

Assumptions Underlying Early Inclusion: The Case for Evidence-Based Practices The benefits described earlier assume two things:

1. Inclusive services begin at an early age and continue through secondary school.
2. These benefits are derived from programs that utilize *evidence-based practices.*

It is imperative that programs orchestrate inclusion in an intentional manner, guided by practices that are known to work (refer to Chapter 1). We learned in Chapter 2 that federal law guides inclusive services. We also learned that the type of services children receive and the setting(s) in which they receive them are outlined in each eligible child's IEP. Each IEP team, which includes parents, reviews assessment results to identify long-term goals for each child (e.g., cooperative play—social and communication domains) and short-term objectives that guide the child's incremental progress (e.g., requesting toys from a peer, turn-taking) toward identified goals. For instance, if a 5-year old child with social and communication delays is eligible for special education services, her IEP team might feel it is important that she be able to play cooperatively with friends before she begins kindergarten the following year. If she is unable to request toys from a peer or take turns, however, she will not be able to achieve this goal. So the team creates short-term goals addressing these more specific skills, also enabling team members to monitor her progress toward her overall goal. Two things are inherent in this planning: 1) an understanding of child development and 2) an understanding of *how* to promote specific outcomes. Team members must participate in a collaborative decision-making process that considers evidence about the child's development, her needs, family priorities for the child, and practices that will successfully support her progress toward identified goals—we call this process *evidence-based practice.*

Described by Buysse, Wesley, Snyder, and Winton (2006) *evidence-based practice* empowers professionals (and parents) to make informed decisions about how best to support young children. If parents want their child to be able to play with her peers, we as professionals must know under what conditions (e.g., environment) and with which practices (e.g., LEAP program model) we can facilitate her cooperative play skills. *Similarly, if we aim to help children achieve the outcomes described here and later in this chapter, we must know how to promote these skills.* For this, we rely on evidence—research, professional wisdom, and family priorities and values—about high-quality early childhood settings, effective instructional practices, and useful communication and collaboration strategies between teachers and professionals that will individually and collectively promote her success.

Evidence-based practice should inform any preschool inclusion effort. Three sets of practices—practices to design a high-quality environment, practices to promote the outcomes described in this chapter, and strategies to foster staff and family collaboration—are immediately relevant to building an inclusive program. High-quality preschool environments meet a series of research-driven standards that promote child safety, learning, and growth. These standards are described in Chapter 4, along with strategies to assess your program's "readiness" for inclusion. Instructional practices, such as embedded intervention or assistive technology, provide children with opportunities to acquire new skills through meaningful and relevant activities and experiences. Embedded interventions, for instance, are designed intentionally to facilitate children with disabilities' meaningful participation in daily routines (Snyder,

Hemmeter, Sandall, & McLean, 2007). Assistive technology is another instructional practice used to support a variety of developmental and functional skills in early childhood (Dunst, Trivette, Hamby, & Simkus, 2013). Though outside the scope of this book, we felt it was important to point readers toward these and other effective practices in early childhood. In Quick Tips 3.1, we direct you to resources about instructional practices and how to use them to increase staff learning and competence.

Finally, in Chapter 6, we describe how to effectively engage staff and families in considering and building an inclusive program. We present a systematic approach to garner buy-in around inclusion and to facilitate the collaborative culture needed to make inclusion work. As you continue to read, remember that decisions based on little or no research and professional support, or decisions that disregard family priorities, are likely to do more harm than good for children's learning and success.

It is imperative that programs orchestrate inclusion in an intentional manner, guided by practices that are known to work.

INCLUSION BENEFITS FOR TYPICALLY DEVELOPING CHILDREN

Building Blocks of Social Skills

It is Shaun's 1st day of school. Like many parents, Shaun's parents are nervous that he might have a hard time fitting in and making friends. Three-year-old Shaun is shy and does not always know how to get his peers to interact with him. Shortly after arrival, the children are given a chance to play at centers. Shaun naturally navigates toward the blocks because he enjoys building things. While at the block station, Shaun encounters Adi, a child who also enjoys playing with the blocks.

Initially, Shaun and Adi have limited interaction. Over several weeks, however, Shaun and Adi begin to share blocks with one another. Their interaction begins wordlessly as they reach for the same block in a pile purposely placed by their teachers to encourage their interaction. Their teachers use these interactions as opportunities to teach and encourage Shaun and Adi's use of positive and appropriate socials skills. When Adi needs a block that Shaun is using, the teacher prompts Adi to ask Shaun for the block.

QUICK TIPS 3.1

Searching for Evidence-Based Practices to Support Inclusion in the Classroom

- **Subscribe to professional and academic journals.** Some journals are available online at no cost (e.g., *Early Childhood Research and Practice*), whereas others may be accessed with professional organizational memberships (e.g., *Young Exceptional Children, Teaching Young Children*). Select 1–2 that are most relevant to your program and subscribe to them. Every other month, invite staff members to select an article describing an effective practice, review it, and then discuss the practice at a staff meeting.
- **Attend conferences and workshops.** Budgeting for staff to attend national and local conferences that address inclusion is useful, though it may not be possible with impending cuts to early education. Fortunately, conference planners are increasingly posting presentations online. Search for relevant topics, download materials, and share them with staff.
    - Early Childhood Inclusion Institute (http://inclusioninstitute.fpg.unc.edu)
    - Division for Early Childhood (DEC) Annual Conference on Children with Special Needs and Their Families (http://www.dec-sped.org/Conference)
    - National Association for the Education of Young Children (NAEYC; http://www.naeyc.org/conference)
- **Build professional development activities around reputable online resources.** Encourage or require staff to complete online training modules specifically designed to support the use of evidence-based instructional practices. One widely used resource is CONNECT: The Center to Mobilize Early Childhood Knowledge: http://community.fpg.unc.edu/. Modules focus on embedded interventions, transition, communication for collaboration, family–professional partnerships, assistive technology, dialogic reading, and tiered interventions.
- **Explore local resources.** Children are best served when there is a network of people working to improve their

development. Luckily, many resources are available to professionals to create this community of support.

- Search for high-quality inclusive preschool programs in your neighborhood or district. Coordinate multiple opportunities for your staff to observe inclusion in action.
- Seek the consultation of community college and university professors who specialize in inclusion.
- Budget for staff to take coursework at a local college or university.
- Engage the community in programs focused on peer-mentoring relationships to encourage teachers to share, observe, and reflect on useful practices.

With verbal cues, time, and teacher reinforcement, Adi learns to independently ask Shaun for a block. By midyear, Adi and Shaun have become quite the construction team! By the end of the year, both Adi and Shaun are showing improved social interaction skills and are sharing many more toys with each other and their classmates independently!

At the preschool's year-end party, Shaun's and Adi's parents meet. Shaun's parents express how happy they are that Shaun has found a friend that helped him overcome his shyness to approach and ask peers to play. Shaun's mom shares that Shaun now asks children he does not know to play also! Much to their surprise, Adi's parents express similar enthusiasm. Little did Shaun's parents know that Adi had an IFSP (refer to Chapter 2). They openly share with Shaun's parents that initiating interactions and sharing were two goals on Adi's IFSP. She is showing tremendous growth as a result of her interactions with Shaun and her teachers' focused intervention.

As you will read later, it is through peer-to-peer interactions and adult guidance that all children can benefit from inclusion. Adi, a child with an IFSP, benefited from the peer interaction, thus making gains in her IFSP goal areas, as did Shaun, a typically developing child who learned how to initiate conversation, share toys, and sustain play. These gains are the result of the teacher knowing how to intentionally facilitate interactions in ways appropriate to the child's developmental levels. In other words, the teacher used *evidence-based practice* to structure Shaun and Adi's environment and interaction to promote both of their abilities.

As an administrator considering inclusion, one of the major questions you will face is, How will the inclusion of children with disabilities affect the typically developing children in the classroom? This is an important and valid question to begin with and one many parents and practitioners share (Rafferty & Griffin, 2005).

How will the inclusion of children with disabilities affect the typically developing children in the classroom?

It is true that much inclusion research has focused on how inclusion can influence and have an impact on the developmental outcomes for children with disabilities. And until recently, there was little evidence to state definitively that including children with disabilities is not in some way negatively affecting those children's typical peers. There is now sufficient evidence to suggest that typical peers are not harmed by or disadvantaged in inclusive classrooms; rather, they grow and develop as a result of the relationships they cultivate and sustain with their diverse counterparts (Buysse & Bailey, 1993; Odom et al., 2004). The following sections again review the immediate and then long-term benefits of inclusion for those peers, whom teachers and parents often rely on to model and scaffold developmentally appropriate behaviors for their classmates with disabilities.

Immediate Benefits

Typically developing children learn a great deal from their classmates with disabilities in inclusive settings. First, the mere inclusion of children with disabilities prompts typical peers to become more understanding of and to develop positive attitudes toward their diverse counterparts (Odom & Bailey, 2001). One of the more cited advantages revolves around the repeated and impromptu interactions that can occur in an inclusive environment (Odom et al., 2002). When children with disabilities or differing abilities attempt to engage their typical peers in social interaction, typically developing children learn to respond to these initiations and thus take further action in the following ways:

- Initiate interactions
- Negotiate sharing
- Develop an understanding of other children (Odom et al., 2002)

Inclusion of children with disabilities prompts typical peers to become more understanding of and to develop positive attitudes toward their diverse counterparts.

In addition, typical peers can learn to identify targeted ways to engage peers with differing abilities (Tsao et al., 2008). More recently, Diamond and Hong (2010) found that typically developing children are also more likely to approach their decisions to include children with disabilities in play based on fairness and equity. Their study, which took place in several preschool classrooms that included children with physical delays, revealed that children are more likely to include peers when activities are less demanding motorically, suggesting that teachers can design a classroom to naturally facilitate the active involvement of all preschoolers with and without disabilities.

Teachers can design a classroom to naturally facilitate the active involvement of all preschoolers with and without disabilities.

In addition to experiencing improved prosocial behaviors, typical peers may also be given the opportunity to become experts in academic areas. There is strong evidence to support the notion that children who are able to model exemplary behaviors to their fellow classmates are likely to demonstrate a heightened level of ability in these activities (Katz & Chard, 2000). As children do this, they are also likely to show increased

- Self-esteem
- Confidence

- Autonomy
- Leadership skills

Imagine the boost in importance a child will feel when he or she serves as an expert on a topic valued by his or her peers.

With a strengthened sense of self, and as they get older, typical peers can move into a tutoring role with proper teacher support (Fuchs, Fuchs, & Burish, 2000; Scruggs & Mastropieri, 1998). Typically developing children who have a strong grasp of content and materials are ideal for this role and can work with peers to facilitate their learning of course material (Scruggs & Mastropieri, 1998). Peer tutoring enables typical children to continue to explain concepts, subsequently mastering subject matter (Fuchs et al., 2000). As a result, typical peers continue to build their self-esteem and sustain positive feelings toward individuals with disabilities. Thus this peer-support model leads to a better-managed classroom in which all students can benefit (Scruggs & Mastropieri, 1998). Further, students approach course material and school overall with more enthusiasm.

Longer Term Benefits

The research on longer term benefits of inclusion for typical peers is limited but also continues to emerge. There is some evidence to suggest that typical peers experience little academic advancement as a result of being paired with younger classmates with disabilities (Odom et al., 2004). Although more research on this phenomenon is needed, typical peers do not lose skills as a result of these interactions, a myth commonly associated with inclusion (see Strain & Bovey, 2011).

When children are exposed to inclusion at an early age and consistently throughout their lives, they are more likely to approach children with disabilities with acceptance (Rafferty et al., 2001) and are less likely to view a disability as an impairment (Burnstein, Sears, Wilcoxen, Cabello, & Spagna, 2004; Idol, 2006). Typical peers are also willing to initiate and maintain friendships with children who may be different and to assist classmates who may be experiencing difficulty with school-related tasks (Burnstein et al., 2004; Idol, 2006). Researchers have also found that some children even learn to adjust their communication without teacher instruction to engage their classmates who communicate differently than they do (Guralnick & Paul-Brown, 1977). Collectively, these positive behaviors improve the atmosphere and generate a sense of collegiality within the classroom and across the school.

When children are exposed to inclusion at an early age and consistently throughout their lives, they are more likely to approach children with disabilities with acceptance.

Though children introduced to inclusion at an early age view inclusion favorably (Idol, 2006), older children's willingness to accept and include peers with disabilities may wane. In fact, evidence suggests that older children are less likely to be receptive of children with disabilities being included in academic settings (Siperstein, Parker, Bardon, & Widaman, 2007). Siperstein and colleagues surveyed 7th- and 8th-grade students of 47 districts from 26 states. In this nationally representative sample, students thought including students with disabilities would improve their attitudes toward people with disabilities but that inclusion would negatively affect academic outcomes. More specifically, the surveyed students thought children with disabilities would take up more teacher attention than what is "typical" and lead to lower academic performance in the class as a whole. Finally, typically developing students were not likely to be interested in associating with children with disabilities outside of school (Siperstein et al., 2007). The students from Siperstein and colleagues' research were from a spectrum of inclusive models, and their views on the role of children with disabilities in the classroom were in contrast to students from fully inclusive models (Burnstein et al., 2004; Idol, 2006). Thus it is our belief that inclusion is in the best interests of all children and is most effective when enacted as early as possible, when children are still open to the concept of inclusion.

Inclusion is in the best interests of all children and is most effective when enacted as early as possible.

CONCLUDING THOUGHTS

As you can see, the evidence supporting the inclusion of children with disabilities is plentiful and growing. Hopefully a few things are evident to you after reading this chapter:

1. There is no evidence to suggest that inclusion leads to decreased academic, social, or later life outcomes.

2. Children with disabilities benefit from being included in the general education classroom in both the short and the long term.
3. Evidence-based practices should guide decisions to support children's outcomes across settings.
4. Typically developing children show benefits while participating in inclusive settings.

Chapter 6 suggests strategies to use this information to gain the support of your staff, families, and any practitioners and colleagues you may work with to implement inclusion.

REFERENCES

Antia, S.D., & Levine, L.M. (2001). Educating deaf and hearing children together: Confronting the challenges of inclusion. In M. Guralnick (Ed.), *Early childhood inclusion: Focus on change* (pp. 365–398). Baltimore, MD: Paul H. Brookes Publishing Co.

Bailey, D.B., McWilliams, R.A., Buysse, V., & Wesley, P.W. (1998). Inclusion in the context of competing values in early childhood education. *Early Childhood Research Quarterly, 13,* 27–47.

Banda, D.R., Hart, S.L., & Liu-Gitz, L. (2010). Impact of training peers and children with autism on social skills during center time activities in inclusive classrooms. *Research in Autism Spectrum Disorders, 4,* 619–625.

Barnett, W.S., Carolan, M.E., Fitzgerald, J., & Squires, J.H. (2011). *The state of preschool 2011: State preschool yearbook.* New Brunswick, NJ: National Institute for Early Education Research. Retrieved from http://nieer.org/sites/nieer/files/2011yearbook.pdf

Barnett, W.S., & Hustedt, J.T. (2011). *Policy brief: Improving public financing for early learning programs.* The National Institute for Early Education Research. Retrieved from http://nieer.org/resources/policybriefs/24.pdf

Brigance, A. (1991). *Brigance diagnostic inventory of early development* (Rev. ed.). North Billerica, MA: Curriculum Associates.

Brigham, N., Morocco, C.C., Clay, K., & Zigmond, N. (2006). What makes a high school a good high school for students with disabilities. *Learning Disabilities Research and Practice, 21,* 184–190.

Burnstein, N., Sears, S., Wilcoxen, A., Cabello, B., & Spagna, M. (2004). Moving toward inclusive practices. *Remedial and Special Education, 25,* 104–116.

Buysse, V., & Bailey, D.B. (1993). Behavioral and developmental outcomes in young children with disabilities in integrated and segregated settings: A review of comparative studies. *Journal of Special Education, 26,* 434–461.

Buysse, V., Goldman, B.D., & Skinner, M.L. (2003). Friendship formation in inclusive early childhood classrooms: What is the teacher's role? *Early Childhood Research Quarterly, 18,* 485–501.

Buysse, V., & Hollingsworth, H.L. (2009). Research synthesis points on early childhood inclusion: What every practitioner and all families should know. *Young Exceptional Children Monograph Series No. 11,* 18–30.

Buysse, V., Wesley, P.W., Snyder, P., & Winton, P. (2006). Evidence-based practice: What does it really mean for the early childhood field? *Young Exceptional Children, 9*(4), 2–11.

Cawley, J.F., Hayden, S., Cade, E., & Baker-Kroczynski, S. (2002). Including students with disabilities into the general education science classroom. *Exceptional Children, 68,* 423–435.

DeSimone, J.R., & Parmar, R.S. (2006). Middle school mathematics teachers' beliefs about inclusion of students with learning disabilities. *Learning Disabilities Research and Practice, 21,* 98–110.

Diamond, K.E., & Hong, S.-Y. (2010). Young children's decisions to include peers with physical disabilities in play. *Journal of Early Intervention, 32,* 163–177.

Dunst, C., Trivette, C., Hamby, D., & Simkus, A. (2013). Systematic review of studies promoting the use of assistive technology devices by young children with disabilities. *Tots-n-Tech Research Brief, 8*(1), 1–21.

Early Childhood Outcomes Center. (n.d.-a). Federal requirements: OSEP requirements: Reporting on child outcomes and the family indicator. Retrieved from http://projects.fpg.unc.edu/~eco/pages/fed_req.cfm

Early Childhood Outcomes Center. (n.d.-b). Outcomes FAQ. Retrieved from http://projects.fpg.unc.edu/~eco/pages/faqs_view_item.cfm?id=12

Eisenman, L.T., & Tascione, L. (2002). "How come nobody told me?": Fostering self-realization through a high school English curriculum. *Learning Disabilities Research and Practice, 17,* 35–46.

Epstein, A.S. (2008). *The intentional teacher: Choosing the best strategies for young children's learning.* Washington, DC: National Association for the Education of Young Children.

Fuchs, D., Fuchs, L., & Burish, P. (2000). Peer-assisted learning strategies: An evidence-based practice to promote reading achievement. *Learning Disabilities Research and Practice, 15,* 85–91.

Goldstein, H. (1993). Structuring environmental input to facilitate generalized language learning by children with mental retardation. In A.P. Kaiser & D.B. Gray (Eds.), *Enhancing children's communication: Research foundations for intervention* (pp. 317–334). Baltimore, MD: Paul H. Brookes Publishing Co.

Guralnick, M.J. (1990). Early childhood mainstreaming. *Topics in Early Childhood Special Education, 2,* 1–17.

Guralnick, M.J. (2001). Social competence with peers and early childhood inclusion: Need for alternative approaches. In M. Guralnick (Ed.), *Early childhood inclusion: Focus on change* (pp. 481–502). Baltimore, MD: Paul H. Brookes Publishing Co.

Guralnick, M.J., & Paul-Brown, D. (1977). The nature of verbal interactions among handicapped and nonhandicapped preschool children. *Child Development, 48,* 254–260.

Hart, B., & Risley, T.R. (1995). *Meaningful differences in the everyday experience of young American children.* Baltimore, MD: Paul H. Brookes Publishing Co.

Holahan, A., & Costenbader, V. (2000). A comparison of developmental gains for preschool children with disabilities in inclusive and self-contained classrooms. *Topics in Early Childhood Special Education, 20,* 224–235.

Hoyson, M., Jamieson, B., & Strain, P.S. (1985). Individualized group instruction of normally developing and autistic-like children: The LEAP curriculum model. *Journal of the Division for Early Childhood, 8,* 157–172.

Hughes, C., Carter, E.W., Hughes, T., Bradford, E., & Copeland, S.R. (2002). Effects of instructional versus non-instructional roles on the social interactions of high school students. *Education and Training in Mental Retardation and Development Disabilities, 37,* 262–272.

Idol, L. (2006). Toward inclusion of special education students in general education: A program evaluation of eight schools. *Remedial and Special Education, 27,* 77–94.

Katz, L.G., & Chard, S. (2000). *Engaging children's minds: The project approach.* Norwood, NJ: Ablex Publishing.

Lamorey, S., & Bricker, D. (1992). Integrated programs: Effects on young children and their parents. In C.A. Peck, S.L. Odom, & D. Bricker (Eds.), *Integrating young children with disabilities into community programs: From research to implementation* (pp. 249–279). Baltimore, MD: Paul H. Brookes Publishing Co.

National Institute for Early Education Research (NIEER). (2012, April). *Pre-K spending per child drops to levels of nearly a decade ago* [news release]. Retrieved from http://nieer.org/news-events/news-releases/pre-k-spending-child-drops-levels-nearly-decade-ago

National Professional Development Center on Autism Spectrum Disorders. (2010, October). *Evidence-base for peer-mediated instruction and intervention* [fact sheet]. Retrieved from http://autismpdc.fpg.unc.edu/sites/autismpdc.fpg.unc.edu/files/PMII_EvidenceBase.pdf

National Professional Development Center on Inclusion (NPDCI). (2009). *Research synthesis points on early childhood inclusion.* Chapel Hill: University of North Carolina, Frank Porter Graham (FPG) Child Development Institute, Author. Retrieved from http://npdci.fpg.unc.edu/sites/npdci.fpg.unc.edu/files/resources/NPDCIResearchSynthesisPoints-10-2009_0.pdf

Odom, S.L. (2000). Preschool inclusion: What we know and where to go from here. *Topics in Early Childhood Special Education, 20,* 20–27.

Odom, S.L., & Bailey, D. (2001). Inclusive preschool programs: Classroom ecology and child outcomes. In M. Guralnick (Ed.), *Early childhood inclusion: Focus on change* (pp. 253–276). Baltimore, MD: Paul H. Brookes Publishing Co.

Odom, S.L., Vitztum, J., Wolery, R., Lieber, J., Sandall, S., Hanson, M.J., Beckman, P., Schwartz, I., & Horn, E. (2004). Preschool inclusion in the United States: A review of research from an ecological systems perspective. *Journal of Research in Special Education Needs, 41,* 17–49.

Odom, S.L., Zercher, C., Marquart, J., Li, S., Sandall, S.R., & Wolfberg, P. (2002). Social relationships of children with disabilities and their peers in inclusive preschool classrooms. In S.L. Odom (Ed.), *Widening the circle: Including children with disabilities in preschool programs* (pp. 61–80). New York, NY: Teachers College Press.

Paul-Brown, D., & Caperton, C.J. (2001). Inclusive practices for preschool-age children with specific language impairment. In M. Guralnick (Ed.), *Early childhood inclusion: Focus on change* (pp. 433–464). Baltimore, MD: Paul H. Brookes Publishing Co.

Peters, S. (2004). *Inclusive education an EFA strategy for all children.* Washington, DC: World Bank.

Rafferty, Y., Boettcher, C., & Griffin, K.W. (2001). Benefits and risks of reverse inclusion for preschoolers with and without disabilities: Parents' perspectives. *Journal of Early Intervention, 24,* 266–286.

Rafferty, Y., & Griffin, K.W. (2005). Benefits and risks of reverse inclusion for preschoolers with and without disabilities: Perspectives of parents and providers. *Journal of Early Intervention, 27,* 173–192. doi:10.1177/105381510502700305

Sandall, S.R., & Schwartz, I.S. (2008). *Building blocks for teaching preschoolers with special needs* (2nd ed.). Baltimore, MD: Paul H. Brookes Publishing Co.

Scruggs, T.E., & Mastropieri, M.A. (1998). Peer tutoring and students with special needs. In K. Topping & S. Ehly (Eds.), *Peer-assisted learning* (pp. 165–182). Mahwah, NJ: Lawrence Erlbaum.

Siperstein, G.N., Parker, R.C., Bardon, J.N., & Widaman, K.F. (2007). A national study of youth attitudes toward the inclusion of students with intellectual disabilities. *Exceptional Children, 73,* 435–455.

Snyder, P., Hemmeter, M.L., Sandall, S., & McLean, M. (2007). *Research summary on embedded interventions.* Retrieved from http://community.fpg.unc.edu/connect-modules/learners/module-1

Strain, P.S. (1983). Generalization of autistic children's social behavior change: Effects of developmentally integrated and segregated settings. *Analysis and Intervention in Developmental Disabilities, 3,* 23–24.

Strain, P.S., & Bovey, E.H. (2011). Randomized, controlled trial of the LEAP model of early intervention for young children with autism spectrum disorders. *Topics in Early Childhood Special Education, 31,* 133–154. doi:10.1177/0271121411408740

Strain, P.S., Bovey, E.H., Wilson, K., & Roybal, R. (2009). LEAP preschool: Lessons learned over 28 years of inclusive services for young children with autism. *Young Exceptional Children Monograph Series No. 11,* 49–68.

Strain, P.S., & Hoyson, M. (2000). On the need for longitudinal intensive social skills training. *Topics in Early Childhood Special Education, 20,* 116–122.

Strain, P.S., McGee, G.G., & Kohler, F.W. (2001). Inclusion of children with autism in early intervention environments: An examination of rationale, myths, and procedures. In M. Guralnick (Ed.), *Early childhood inclusion: Focus on change* (pp. 337–364). Baltimore, MD: Paul H. Brookes Publishing Co.

Tsao, L.L., Odom, S.L., Buysse, V., Skinner, M., West, T., & Vitztum-Komanecki, J. (2008). Social participation of children with disabilities in inclusive preschool programs: Program typology and ecological features. *Exceptionality, 16,* 125–140.

U.S. Department of Education, Office of Special Education and Rehabilitative Services, Office of Special Education Programs. (2011). *30th annual report to congress on the implementation of the Individuals with Disabilities Education Act, 2008.* Washington, DC: Author.

Wiener, J., & Tardif, C.Y. (2004). Social and emotional functioning of children with learning disabilities: Does special education placement make a difference? *Learning Disabilities Research and Practice, 19,* 20–32.

Wilson, G.L., & Michaels, C.A. (2006). General and special education students' perceptions of co-teaching: Implications for secondary-level literacy instruction. *Reading and Writing Quarterly: Overcoming Learning Difficulties, 22,* 205–225.

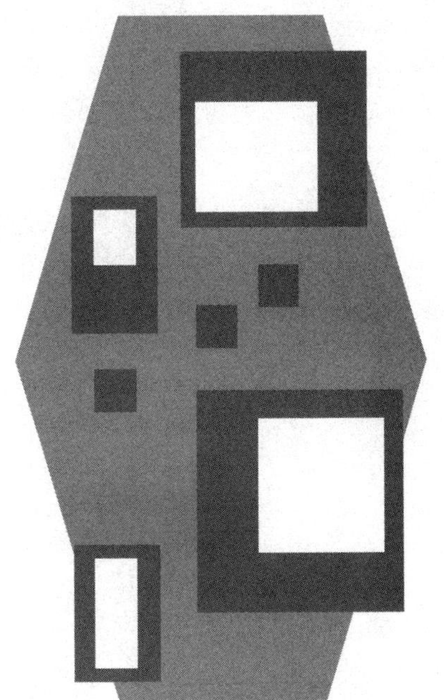

SECTION II

Critical Considerations for Inclusion

CHAPTER 4

Is My Program Ready for Inclusion?

Assessing the Climate

Sarika S. Gupta

"I'm ready for inclusion, but I'm not sure my program is."

Nan is a private preschool director and a mother of a 9-year-old with a learning disability. Nan's preschool center serves children from birth through 8 years old, and she is very interested in including children with disabilities. Her son was diagnosed with developmental delay at the age of 4, and she has seen firsthand how he benefited from being around his typically developing friends. Thinking back, she also remembers feeling that his friends developed a greater sensitivity to the learning differences in others as a result of being around him. Nan believes strongly in inclusion; however, she feels she does not have specialized knowledge of disabilities or teaching skills to support it as a daily practice. Moreover, she worries about whether her staff will be receptive to inclusion, as many of them are not familiar with disabilities.

Nan decided to pursue a graduate degree in ECSE. She hopes to learn more about the laws that govern inclusion, the evidence supporting inclusion, and practical strategies to engage children with diverse abilities in meaningful ways. She suspects that inclusion largely entails individualizing instruction. She is surprised to learn during her studies that successful inclusion relies on a number of other features, for example, a high-quality classroom. Such a classroom is staffed with knowledgeable teachers, is safe, and meets environmental standards, such as teacher-to-child ratios. A high-quality classroom will offer children the right mix of structured and unstructured opportunities to facilitate child learning in developmentally appropriate and culturally and linguistically sensitive ways. Nan also learns that staff support is critical to the success of inclusion. Staff that are involved in the decision-making process are more likely to feel empowered and capable of providing individualized instruction to children with varying needs. Finally, she learns that families make all the difference. Families have specific priorities for their children. Engaging them as partners in the decision-making process is one way to acknowledge families' unique perspectives and to build community support for a program that addresses their children's collective abilities and needs.

As Nan learns that inclusion requires not only specialized knowledge but also critical administrative support and buy-in from the community, she feels she has a better understanding of what is needed. She wants to take a closer look at her program to see what she can do as an administrator to kick-start her inclusion efforts.

Recall from Chapter 1 that *inclusion* means providing children with disabilities routine and meaningful opportunities to interact with typically developing children to the maximum extent possible. This chapter examines the components that can facilitate such high-quality interactions, beginning with the classroom environment. Several resources in the field, developed by the NAEYC and Division of Early Childhood (DEC) of the Council for Exceptional Children, highlight these components and are presented first.

We then reflect on Nan's situation from the beginning of the chapter to consider the collaborative relationships needed to implement inclusion on a day-to-day basis. Inclusion requires teamwork; as the leader, you will need the support of others daily. From research it is clear that inclusion efforts are likely to be successful when staff and families are on board (Beckman et al., 1998; Lieber et al., 2000). You, as the leader of this effort, will need to gauge the interest of your staff and families, likely educate them about inclusion and its benefits, and enlist their assistance to build a vision for and to carry out inclusion every day. Being aware of potential concerns will help you identify potential needs areas. Use this chapter to assess your program's readiness and to identify needs. For additional examples of staff and family needs and barriers to inclusion, refer to Chapter 7. Before reading on, visit Activity Corner 4.1 to reflect on whether Nan's classroom will support inclusion.

Inclusion requires teamwork.

ACTIVITY CORNER 4.1
Reflect and Discuss

Review the vignette at the beginning of the chapter. Identify the features that will support inclusion that Nan is surprised to learn about. Discuss how the absence of each feature might hinder inclusion.

ASSESSING PROGRAM QUALITY

"High quality programs regularly evaluate their own performance" (Hemmeter, Sandall, & Smith, 2005, p. 243).

Inclusion alone does not equate to high quality, nor does high quality necessarily mean inclusion is practiced (Schwartz, Sandall, Odom, Horn, & Beckman, 2002). Determining whether your program is of good quality is a great way to begin your effort. The setting should be safe for all children, be equipped with meaningful and appropriate materials, contain adequate space, and employ well-trained and educated staff. The next step involves examining day-to-day practices, for example, between administrators and teachers, between teachers and children, and even between children! What practices are in place? Are these practices supported by research (see discussion of evidence-based practices in Chapter 3)? Do the practices work, meaning do the practices lead children to achieve positive outcomes? If not, is there a sound rationale in place for their use? This section reviews standards for the environment, practices, and programs that have been shown to support young children's development. Take a moment now to reflect on your own program's quality by completing Activity Corner 4.2.

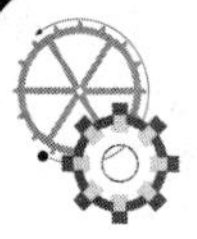

ACTIVITY CORNER 4.2
Reflect and Discuss

With a partner or colleague, describe the ways in which your program assesses quality. To start, think about child safety, space, staffing, materials, and practices. Note additional characteristics as you discuss with each other.

Determining whether your program is of good quality is a great way to begin.

After her course, Nan reflects on the quality of classrooms within her program. Until now, she had thought she was doing everything she could to ensure the safety of her students. The program met licensing standards, so she was confident that her classrooms were safe, inviting spaces that were staffed with well-trained adults and filled with materials her young students would enjoy. However, through her graduate coursework, Nan learns about many more resources she can use to enhance the quality of the program and that program quality involves so much more than simply the classroom environment! One resource is NAEYC. Several of her graduate student colleagues mention using NAEYC resources to guide environmental design in their schools. Through class activities, she also learns about DEC of the Council for Exceptional Children. Because of time constraints, she and her colleagues are not able to meet during the academic year, but they decide to schedule monthly coffee times during the summer to talk about resources they are using to improve their programs. As the first meeting approaches, Nan decides to look up NAEYC and DEC. Through a brief search, she learns that they are both professional organizations in early childhood. She wonders: Why are there two organizations for this purpose? And how are they different, if at all?

PROGRAMMATIC CONSIDERATIONS: PROGRAM QUALITY

We focus first on an observable characteristic of inclusion: *the setting*. Preschool inclusion typically takes place in community-based settings such as a state-funded preschool program, a Head Start classroom, or in child care. Private programs, faith-based programs, and family child care settings may also implement inclusion. Regardless of where inclusion occurs, each setting should meet 10 standards, described in FYI 4.1, for high-quality care and education. These standards were developed by NAEYC and enable programs to seek national accreditation, an index for program quality in early childhood. Pause here to complete Activity Corner 4.3 and then continue reading.

Regardless of where inclusion occurs, each setting should meet 10 standards for high-quality care and education.

The Council for Exceptional Children's DEC focuses on a second observable characteristic of inclusion: *practices*. Mounting evidence from the field continues to show the link between early experience and positive outcomes in behavior, health, and learning. Many of the practices known to be effective in promoting these favorable outcomes are summarized in DEC's recommended practices guidebook. Described more fully in a section later in this chapter, these include direct practices (e.g., assessment, child-focused practices;

FYI 4.1

National Association for the Education of Young Children Accreditation Standards

1. Relationships
2. Curriculum
3. Teaching
4. Assessment of child progress
5. Health
6. Teachers
7. Families
8. Community relationships
9. Physical environment
10. Leadership and management

ACTIVITY CORNER 4.3

What Is the National Association for the Education of Young Children and What Are Its Aims?

NAEYC is a leading worldwide organization of professionals working on behalf of young children from birth through age 8. Visit http://www.naeyc.org to answer the following questions:

- What does the abbreviation NAEYC stand for?
- What is NAEYC's mission/vision?
- Describe NAEYC's membership.
- What areas and topics does NAEYC address in ECE?
- Who should get involved in NAEYC and why?
- Who benefits as a result of NAEYC's work?
- After you explore areas and topics, list three that are of most relevance to your program:
  - ______________________________
  - ______________________________
  - ______________________________

family-based practices; interdisciplinary models; and technology applications) and indirect practices (e.g., policies, procedures, and systems change) that, when implemented well and with consideration of cultural and linguistic diversity and appropriate environmental supports, will help children and families experience positive outcomes. When reviewed collectively, the DEC recommended practices also enable a program to assess its overall approach to supporting young children with special needs. Learn more about DEC in Activity Corner 4.4 before reading onward.

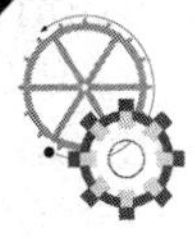

ACTIVITY CORNER 4.4

What Is the Division for Early Childhood and What Are Its Aims?

DEC is an international organization focused on promoting the policies and evidence-based practices that support young children with special needs and their families. Visit http://www.dec-sped.org to answer the following questions:

- What does the abbreviation DEC stand for?
- What is DEC's mission/vision?
- Describe DEC's membership.
- What areas and topics does DEC address in ECE?
- Who should get involved in DEC and why?
- Who benefits as a result of DEC's work?
- After you explore areas and topics, list three that are of most relevance to your program:
  - ____________________
  - ____________________
  - ____________________

Finally, we describe a relatively new effort in the field: *quality rating improvement systems* (QRIS), "a systemic approach to assess, improve, and communicate the level of [early childhood program] quality" (Office of Child Care, 2012, p. 1). Programs that meet state-driven QRIS standards demonstrate a level of quality likely to yield favorable outcomes in children. The QRIS movement is gaining momentum across the country and is preparing programs to seek NAEYC accreditation. FYI 4.4 gives more information about QRIS. The next section describes the movement, standards, and its relevance to inclusion.

Programs that meet state-driven QRIS standards demonstrate a level of quality likely to yield favorable outcomes in children.

The National Association for the Education of Young Children and Program Accreditation

NAEYC "serves and acts on behalf of the needs, rights and well-being of all young children with primary focus on the provision of educational and developmental services and resources" (NAEYC, n.d.-a). The organization accomplishes this mission through three goals:

1. Improving professional practice and working conditions in early childhood education.
2. Supporting early childhood programs by working to achieve a high-quality system of early childhood education.
3. Building a high-performing, inclusive organization of groups and individuals who are committed to promoting excellence in early childhood education for all young children. (NAEYC, n.d.-a)

Collectively, these goals equip practitioners and programs with a knowledge base and skill set to develop high-quality early learning experiences that will encourage lifelong learning and promote health and development. What makes a learning experience "high quality"? There are 10 standards, namely, supported by research and best practice (see NAEYC, 2008):

1. *Relationships*—Programs recognize that children benefit from positive relationships with their peers and with adults and from positive relationships between teachers and families. Through these relationships, children learn that they matter in a larger community, which helps them develop a positive sense of self.

2. *Curriculum*—A program's curriculum should intentionally address five domains of development (social, emotional, physical, language, and cognitive) and should be consistent with program goals to promote child learning and development in appropriate ways.

3. *Teaching*—Programs encourage the use of instructional approaches shown to be effective in promoting early learning and development. These approaches should also consider each child's developmental, cultural, and linguistic diversity. Teachers, then, should know how to diversify and individualize

instructional approaches in order to support the unique interests, learning styles, and needs of each child.

4. *Assessment of child progress*—Programs that continuously collect information (in both formal and informal ways and from child observation, families, and practitioners) are able to make informed decisions about how best to guide children's learning.
5. *Health*—Efforts to protect the safety of both children and staff are in place, as are efforts to support children's nutrition and health.
6. *Teachers*—Program staff are qualified, knowledgeable, and professionally committed to supporting both diverse young children and their families.
7. *Families*—The program recognizes the important role families play in young children's lives and encourages staff to build relationships and collaboration with families to support young children's optimal development.
8. *Community relationships*—Programs are aware of and actively connect with individuals and resources in the community that can provide assistance or support to the diverse needs of young children and their families.
9. *Physical environment*—Both indoor and outdoor physical environments in the program are safe, appropriate, well-maintained, and facilitative to children's and staff's learning and development.
10. *Leadership and management*—A strong infrastructure, including strong leaders, is in place to support staff and to implement the policies and procedures needed to effectively manage a high-quality environment and appropriate learning experiences from which both staff and children will learn and grow.

What makes a learning experience "high quality?"

According to NAEYC, the first five standards—*relationships, curriculum, teaching, assessment of child progress,* and *health*—"focus on the advancement of children's learning and development" (see NAEYC, n.d.-b). Standard 6—*teachers*—focuses on teachers and practitioners that deliver instruction in educational settings, whereas Standards

7 and 8 focus on individuals at home and beyond the school environments. How the environment is administered, meaning how it is structured physically (Standard 9) and how the program is managed and led (Standard 10) also influence program quality. It may be helpful to think about these standards in a series of concentric circles that focus on supporting a young child who stands in the center of the circles (see Figure 4.1). This ecological approach (Bronfenbrenner, 1979) helps us identify individuals—teachers, family members, community partners, and administrators—and other influencing factors (e.g., classroom quality, building quality, playground quality, local initiatives) needed to create positive early learning experiences.

NAEYC has identified these elements as defining features of a successful, high-quality early childhood program. Each standard is based on research and has been shown to produce favorable outcomes for young children (NAEYC, n.d.-c). Programs that demonstrate evidence of meeting each of these standards can earn NAEYC accreditation, a national accreditation that identifies a program as including the critical elements needed to provide children with high-quality learning experiences. Eligible for accreditation are center- or school-based programs that serve a minimum of 10 children.

Programs that demonstrate evidence of meeting each of these standards can earn NAEYC accreditation, a national accreditation that identifies a program as including the critical elements needed to provide children with high-quality learning experiences.

The accreditation process is outside of the scope of this book; however, it is important for program leaders to be aware of this measure of quality, particularly because many families search for programs that can offer their children high-quality experiences that will safely and appropriately promote their children's learning. Accreditation requires preparation, but the outcomes outweigh the effort.

Over coffee, Nan is surprised to hear that all three of her colleagues' programs are both state-licensed and NAEYC-accredited! Her big question is, why are both necessary? Until now, she had heard little about accreditation, so she asks her colleagues to

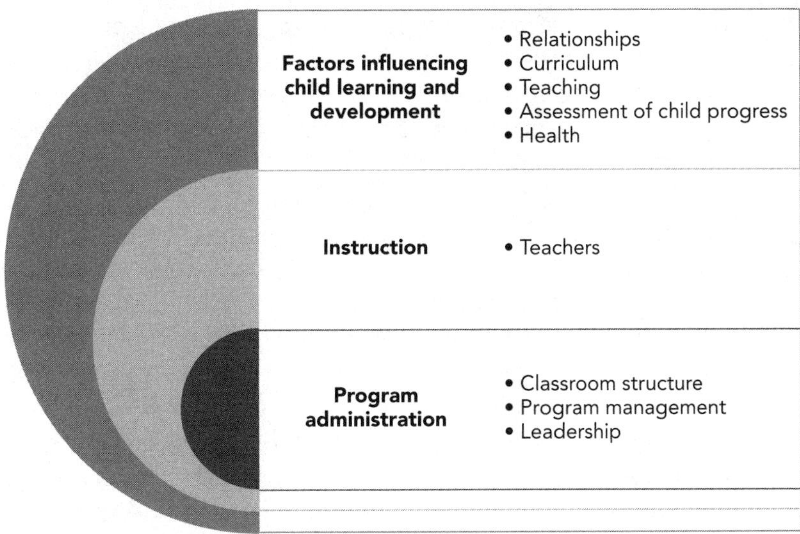

Figure 4.1. Influencing ecological factors.

explain the benefits. They explain that programs use licensing and accreditation to show families that they are addressing the quality features known to help children learn and grow, which makes their programs more reputable. Her colleague Mira describes how many parents ask whether the program is accredited before they decide to enroll their children. She then uses the accreditation to support and increase her enrollment and, therefore, her budget!

Nan's colleague Suri jumps in to describe the benefits to staff. Suri is using the standards to pinpoint where her staff need assistance and professional development. Her accredited program meets all 10 standards; however, several staff have mentioned to her they thought they would benefit from more support in assessing child progress. *They routinely collect data from parent interviews, through observations, and by using research-supported practices (e.g., portfolios, screening), but they felt it was not enough, that these strategies were not helping to capture some of the smaller incremental milestones they knew the children were making. As it turns out, Suri's program includes children with special needs, such as children with diagnoses of developmental delays and autism. As director, Suri knew it was her responsibility to provide professional development to her staff, and, more important, she genuinely wanted to support those teachers who wanted to broaden and improve their skill sets to better guide their young children's learning. One problem, however, was that her budget was tight and the program had already spent the majority of their professional development funds for the year. Suri remembered that her district published a list of NAEYC-accredited programs. Through some brainstorming, she decided to propose a teacher exchange program with a neighboring NAEYC-accredited program. This exchange would provide her teachers with opportunities to observe a program with stronger data collection strategies and to talk with program staff about strategies they have found to be particularly helpful. She, in turn, knew that her program was strong in the* relationships *and* families *components. She knew her staff would be proud to share their approaches in these areas with another program.*

Suri explains to Nan that she really relied on the accreditation to coordinate this exchange, and the teachers were so grateful for this on-the-job support. She goes on to say that when programs have accreditation, she knows that they are aware of the field's standards for quality and that they actively work to implement them to appropriately, safely, and effectively promote child health, development, and learning. See FYI 4.2 for a list of reasons to seek NAEYC accreditation and FYI 4.3 for initial steps toward accreditation.

The Division for Early Childhood and Recommended Practices

DEC is a division of the larger Council for Exceptional Children, an international professional organization committed to ensuring the educational success for children and youth with exceptionalities. Where DEC varies in scope from NAEYC is in its focus on meeting the specific needs of children with disabilities. DEC is a leading

FYI 4.2

Why Seek National Association for the Education of Young Children Accreditation?

- The program will meet research-based standards of high quality.
- Families are more likely to choose your high-quality program.
- Your high-quality program is likely to help children experience positive outcomes and begin school ready to learn.
- Programs with evidence of these positive results are likely to continue receiving funding, support, and resources from local, state, and possibly even national entities.

To learn more about accreditation and to access resources to assist your program in seeking accreditation, visit http://www.naeyc.org/academy.

FYI 4.3

If Your Program Is Not Accredited by the National Association for the Education of Young Children Yet . . .

Some programs are not accredited and may not have the immediate funds to seek accreditation. Leaders in these programs can still begin to assess program quality and inclusion readiness by examining the physical and social characteristics in a classroom or the larger building. Physical characteristics refer to classroom space and arrangement, whereas social characteristics refer to interactions and expectations for children. Research shows that both types of characteristics promote strong learning experiences and social competence in young children (Diamond, Hong, & Baroody, 2007; Odom, Brown, Schwartz, Zercher, & Sandall, 2002). Organize leaders into two groups to complete the activities in Forms 4.1 and 4.2 (see Figures 4.2 and 4.3 for filled-out versions).

presence and the voice of early intervention and early childhood special education. The organization, comprising practitioners, researchers, family members, and policy makers, promotes policies and evidence-based practices that support young children with special needs and their families. The primary vehicle to promote evidence-based practices is the DEC recommended practices guidebook.

> ***DEC is a leading presence and the voice of early intervention and early childhood special education.***

Published in 2005, the DEC recommended practices guidebook is the final product of a concerted effort to encourage the widespread use of *evidence-based practices,* also known as those practices shown to be effective in improving behavior, learning, and development. (See Chapter 3 for a review of evidence-based practices in early childhood.) DEC initiated a systematic review of the literature base, identified practices, and then translated those practices into a series of practical

ASSESSING PHYSICAL CHARACTERISTICS AND INCLUSION READINESS

Certain features of early childhood classrooms have been shown to support children's social and emotional development (Diamond, Hong, & Baroody, 2007).

Step 1: Reflect on the following physical characteristics in a target classroom. List two or three ways each characteristic could support child learning and development in the first column.

Step 2: Review the physical characteristics—do they support children with special needs? List one or two changes you can make to better support a child with a disability. It might be helpful to think about one disability (e.g., physical impairment) to focus your recommended changes.

	Step 1	Step 2
Classroom space	1. 2.	1. 2.
Furniture (e.g., size, arrangement, comfort)	1. 2.	1. 2.
Schedule and routine	1. 2.	1. 2.

Form 4.1. Assessing Physical Characteristics and Inclusion Readiness

ASSESSING PHYSICAL CHARACTERISTICS AND INCLUSION READINESS

	Step 1	Step 2
Centers and activities	1. 2.	1. 2.
Number of adults	1. 2.	1. 2.
Number of children	1. 2.	1. 2.
Ratio of adults to children	1. 2.	1. 2.

ASSESSING PHYSICAL CHARACTERISTICS AND INCLUSION READINESS

Certain features of early childhood classrooms have been shown to support children's social and emotional development (Diamond, Hong, & Baroody, 2007).

Step 1: Reflect on the following physical characteristics in a target classroom. List two or three ways each characteristic could support child learning and development.

Step 2: Review the physical characteristics—do they support a child with special needs? List one or two changes you can make to better support a child with a disability. It might be helpful to think about one disability (e.g., physical impairment) to focus your recommended changes.

	Step 1	Step 2
Classroom space	1. *Classroom is one level (i.e., no steps or gradation in flooring or surface).* 2. *Shelves and tables are used to "partition" the classroom into centers and areas. For example, two shelves enclose the meeting area that is in the corner of the classroom near windows. Students move through the opening between the two shelves (from a linoleum floor onto an industrial carpet) to enter the area, which helps them build an awareness of space and movement.*	1. *Level surface allows for physical accessibility for all children.* 2. *The partitions may limit accessibility and participation for a child with motor issues or physical impairments. Will the opening allow space for a child with crutches or a walker, for example?*
Furniture (e.g., size, arrangement, comfort)	1. *Chairs in the classroom are the same, child-size, plastic, and with a solid back.* 2. *Materials are available for children and within reach if they are sitting or standing. For example, the dramatic play area includes hollow blocks that are stacked on low shelves.*	1. *Including chairs with arms may better support children with postural issues or promote spatial awareness.* 2. *Place some hollow blocks on the floor for more immediate access.*
Schedule and routine	1. *A written schedule is posted on the back of the classroom door.* 2. *The teacher taps a musical wand to alert children to cleanup time and a transition to the next routine.*	1. *Place the schedule in an area that children pass by daily, such as a morning meeting area.* 2. *Provide children who have a hard time with transitions a 2-minute verbal or visual prompt that cleanup will begin shortly and/or invite them to tap the wand after the 2-minute prompt.*

Figure 4.2. Filled-in example of Form 4.1.

ASSESSING PHYSICAL CHARACTERISTICS AND INCLUSION READINESS

	Step 1	Step 2
Centers and activities	1. *There are several centers in the classroom, including a meeting area with books, dramatic play items, sensory objects, manipulatives, and puzzles that children can choose to play with on the carpet or at tables; a writing center; and an art area.* 2. *During morning meeting, all children are expected to sit on a carpet square that the teacher prearranges.*	1. *To promote self-regulation, also include a "quiet" or "cozy" area designed for 1–2 children. Encourage all children to use the area, as they need it.* 2. *For children with postural or attention issues, provide additional seating options, such as a chair with arms or a textured exercise ball.*
Number of adults	1. *There are four adults in the classroom daily: two lead teachers, a paid student assistant, and a student volunteer.* 2. *At arrival time, parents stand in the doorway. Many stay for about 30–45 minutes chatting with one another.*	1. *Great! Are all the adults aware of their roles and responsibilities in the classroom and with the children?* 2. *Welcome parents and gently remind them that the school day will be beginning soon. Placing a schedule near the entrance may be a good way to visually prompt parents that the next routine will begin shortly.*
Number of children	1. *There are 18 children ages 3 and 4 in the class.* 2. *Of the 18, one child expresses challenging behaviors, one child is medically fragile, and one child has speech and language delays.*	1. *Ensure materials and activities are appropriate for a range of abilities, needs, and interests across ages.* 2. *Set aside time during each planning meeting to address supports that will prevent challenging behaviors, physically support the child with medical needs, and address language abilities.*
Ratio of adults to children	1. *There are 18 children and 4 adults.* 2. *On some days, up to two more parents help in the classroom.*	1. *Review state and county licensure requirements to ensure the ratio is appropriate for the ages of children.* 2. *Send home expectations for parent volunteers before they arrive in the classroom, or meet briefly with parents at the beginning of the school day to ensure they understand their role in the classroom.*

ASSESSING SOCIAL CHARACTERISTICS AND INCLUSION READINESS

Certain features of early childhood classrooms have been shown to support children's social and emotional development (Diamond, Hong, & Baroody, 2007).

Step 1: Use these questions to observe the social climate in a target classroom. *Step 2:* As you observe, consider the implications of these characteristics and how they might facilitate or hinder learning, social interaction, and development for a child with a disability. List both positive and negative implications.

	Yes	Somewhat	No	Potential implications for a young child with a disability
Teachers greet children as they arrive.				1. 2.
The classroom follows a schedule or routine.				1. 2.
The schedule or routine is visible to children.				1. 2.
The group size is _____ and seems appropriate for the age group.				1. 2.
The ratio of adults to children is _______ and aligns with licensing regulations.				1. 2.

Form 4.2. Assessing Social Characteristics and Inclusion Readiness

ASSESSING SOCIAL CHARACTERISTICS AND INCLUSION READINESS

	Yes	Somewhat	No	Potential implications for a young child with a disability
Teachers are observing children as they work and play.				1. 2.
Activities and areas support cognitive development.				1. 2.
Opportunities for creative and pretend play are available.				1. 2.
Teachers are engaged with children during work and play.				1. 2.
Teachers are responding to child requests.				1. 2.
Teachers are initiating activities.				1. 2.

(continued)

ASSESSING SOCIAL CHARACTERISTICS AND INCLUSION READINESS

	Yes	Somewhat	No	Potential implications for a young child with a disability
Children are initiating activities.				1. 2.
Children are engaged with materials in the classroom.				1. 2.
Children are engaged with peers in the classroom.				1. 2.
Teachers seem aware of children's needs and abilities.				1. 2.
Teachers regard all children positively.				1. 2.
Teachers seem to anticipate child behaviors and emotions.				1. 2.

ASSESSING SOCIAL CHARACTERISTICS AND INCLUSION READINESS

Certain features of early childhood classrooms have been shown to support children's social and emotional development (Diamond, Hong, & Baroody, 2007).

Step 1: Use these questions to observe the social climate in a target classroom.
Step 2: As you observe, consider the implications of these characteristics and how they might facilitate or hinder learning, social interaction, and development for a child with a disability. List both positive and negative implications.

	Yes	Somewhat	No	Potential implications for a young child with a disability
Teachers greet children as they arrive.		x		1. *Positive—Teachers greet each child verbally at their eye level at morning arrival and wait for a verbal response. Children have also started to greet each other verbally, following the teacher's modeling.* 2. *Negative—Consider the child with language delay. Though present with peers, is he communicating actively and engaged with peers as they greet each other? Maybe provide a series of visuals with emotions so that he can identify and share how he is feeling that day.*
The classroom follows a schedule or routine.	x			1. *Positive—Children expect a consistent daily routine. Teachers refer to the schedule at each transition.* 2. *Negative—None.*
The schedule or routine is visible to children.		x		1. *Positive—The written schedule is posted at children's eye level but behind the door.* 2. *Negative—A written schedule may not be appropriate for all children. Consider including visuals, expanding the print, and moving to a more central location in the classroom so that it is more visible and accessible for children.*
The group size is *18* and seems appropriate for the age group.	x			1. *Positive—Group size is appropriate given licensing guidelines.* 2. *Negative—A larger group size overall may meet licensing guidelines. Consider planning activities that encourage small group interactions so that children have opportunities to participate and interact with peers and teachers.*
The ratio of adults to children is *1:5* and aligns with licensing regulations.	x			1. *Positive—Ratio size is appropriate given licensing guidelines.* 2. *Negative—None. Consider utilizing adults to facilitate small group interactions so that children have opportunities to participate and interact with one another and adults.*

(continued)

Figure 4.3. Filled-in example of Form 4.2.

Figure 4.3. (*continued*)

ASSESSING SOCIAL CHARACTERISTICS AND INCLUSION READINESS

	Yes	Somewhat	No	Potential implications for a young child with a disability
Teachers are observing children as they work and play.	x			1. *Positive—Teachers can gather informal or anecdotal information to learn about children's interests and abilities.* 2. *Negative—None.*
Activities and areas support cognitive development.		x		1. *Positive—Many centers offer children choices.* 2. *Negative—The painting easel offers children only one color and one brush choice. Consider adding another color and a brush with a different size handle to accommodate children's decision making and to provide varied opportunities for fine motor skills.*
Opportunities for creative and pretend play are available.		x		1. *Positive—Dramatic play area is in the classroom (though closed some days).* 2. *Negative—Consider keeping this area open daily as a choice.*
Teachers are engaged with children during work and play.		x		1. *Positive—Some teachers sit with children as they play.* 2. *Negative—Teachers that are seated in close physical proximity to children are not always guiding or scaffolding learning and play.*
Teachers are responding to child requests.		x		1. *Positive—Some teachers sit in close proximity to children at the snack table and facilitate conversations, respond to children's questions, and encourage interactions between children as they request items.* 2. *Negative—Teachers sit on the perimeter of the classroom during free play, often missing vocal or gestural requests for assistance with play or peers.*
Teachers are initiating activities.	x			1. *Positive—Teachers set up several choices for children and then sit beside materials, encouraging children to join them.* 2. *Negative—None.*

ASSESSING SOCIAL CHARACTERISTICS AND INCLUSION READINESS

	Yes	Somewhat	No	Potential implications for a young child with a disability
Children are initiating activities.		*x*		1. *Positive—Children are provided materials that will help them build fine motor and cognitive skills, such as Unifix cubes.* 2. *Negative—Requiring children to use Unifix cubes for patterning may be too limiting. Encouraging children to build towers, modeling patterning of other objects, or praising children's matching of objects throughout the classroom are ways to individualize feedback and scaffold children's learning.*
Children are engaged with materials in the classroom.		*x*		*See "Children are initiating activities" section.*
Children are engaged with peers in the classroom.		*x*		1. *Positive—Mostly yes; however, at the manipulatives table, children are working independently.* 2. *Negative—Although independent exploration should be encouraged, teachers might also encourage peer interactions by modeling how to request items from their peers rather than from the teacher.*
Teachers seem aware of children's needs and abilities.		*x*		1. *Positive—Teachers check in repeatedly with children in the class with physical disabilities and offer them individualized adult support.* 2. *Negative—Although the individualized support and care is positive, it may be shaping peers' perspective of the child as always needing adult assistance.*
Teachers regard all children positively.	*x*			1. *Positive—Teachers interact with children at their eye level, use a positive and enthusiastic tone, and invite children to join in play or activities.* 2. *Negative—None.*
Teachers seem to anticipate child behaviors and emotions.		*x*		1. *Positive—Teachers signal transitions using an aural cue (e.g., magic wand, bell).* 2. *Negative—One child, when engaged in play, consistently does not hear the cue over the sounds of her peers. Peers tell her to clean up suddenly and quickly, which leads her to grow frustrated and then push peers away from her toys. Supplementing the aural cue with a visual cue (e.g., musical wand + lights off) is one way to prevent any agitation and frustration. Alternatively, offering children who need more time with transitions an advance 2-minute warning may be helpful and may prevent potential challenging behaviors.*

recommendations (Sandall & Smith, 2005). This effort, the first of its kind in the field, was driven by three fundamental DEC values:

1. Respect for all children and families
2. High-quality, comprehensive, coordinated, and family-centered services and supports
3. Rights of all children to participate actively and meaningfully within their families and communities. (Sandall, McLean, Santos, & Smith, 2005, pp. 21–24)

Inherent in these values is the understanding that all children matter and that we, as practitioners, should find ways to support each child so that he or she can participate, grow, learn, and succeed in everyday activities and with others. The guidebook, then, offers practical strategies to accomplish this task. Practices are organized by *direct services* and *indirect services*. Direct services address *assessment, child-focused practices, family-based practices,* and *interdisciplinary models.* Indirect supports acknowledge the external factors that enable the delivery of direct services, including *policies, procedures, and systems change,* and *personnel preparation.* Sensitivity to cultural and linguistic diversity is evident across these strands, as are the elements of supportive learning environments. Each strand is self-explanatory and supported with

- A thorough review of the research
- Foundational principles that guide practice
- Recommended practices (see Table 4.1)
- Concrete examples (see Smith, McLean, Sandall, Snyder, & Ramsey, 2005, for a detailed discussion on the procedures and evidence base used to establish each strand)

All children matter, and practitioners should find ways to support each child so that he or she can participate, grow, learn, and succeed in everyday activities and with others.

Table 4.1. Division for Early Childhood Recommended Practices

Direct services strands	Indirect supports strands
Assessment	Policies, procedures, and systems change
Child-focused practices	Personnel preparation
Family-based practices	
Interdisciplinary models	
Technology applications	
Cultural and linguistic diversity and elements for supportive learning environments throughout	

Source: Division for Early Childhood (n.d.).

The research underlying each strand provides a context to understand guiding principles for the practice. What guides *assessment,* for example? After a thorough review of the research, authors Neisworth and Bagnato (2005) assert that assessment in early intervention and preschool special education rests on two principles: *parents as partners* and *developmental appropriateness.* Practitioners should consider this as the foundation from which they conduct their work, outlined by five statements, again supported by evidence:

1. Professionals and families collaborate in planning and implementing assessment.
2. Assessment is individualized and appropriate for the child and family.
3. Assessment provides useful information for intervention.
4. Professionals share information in respectful and useful ways.
5. Professionals meet legal and procedural requirements and Recommended Practices guidelines. (Neisworth & Bagnato, 2005, pp. 49–50)

Following each statement is a series of recommended practices, further described with concrete examples. One of the recommended practices for the first statement ("professionals and families collaborate in planning and implementing assessment") includes the following: *"Families receive a written statement of program philosophy regarding family participation in assessment planning and activities"* (Neisworth & Bagnato, 2005, p. 51). How might programs and practitioners carry out this work?

- A brochure or written statement about family involvement in assessment is provided to families.
- A staff member verbally explains the philosophy of assessment when the brochure or written statement is provided and clarifies any questions the family may have. (p. 51)

Authors use a similar format to describe each strand.

The goal, then, is to provide programs with concrete, empirically supported practices they can use to promote positive developmental and learning outcomes for young children with disabilities and their families (Sandall & Smith, 2005).

Summarizing each strand is outside of the scope of this book; however, it is important for leaders to be aware of this additional and practical resource created specifically to guide program assessment and to encourage program staff to implement effective practices. Like NAEYC standards, DEC recommended practices help programs assess themselves. DEC strands and practices differ from NAEYC standards in that they delve deeper into the specific practices professionals should apply across the continuum of early childhood settings. Think back to the idea of concentric circles with the child in the center. NAEYC standards are the outermost circle guiding the establishment of the overall environment and the overall philosophy and approach to early childhood, whereas the DEC strands and practices, as the inner circle, provide structured and individualized strategies to directly support young children, families, and the professionals working with them. Both NAEYC standards and DEC recommended practices should guide the development of any early childhood program and its day-to-day functioning and performance.

Like NAEYC standards, DEC recommended practices help programs assess themselves.

Summary

Unlike NAEYC accreditation, programs may not seek accreditation for the use of recommended practices. What programs can and should do, however, is use the recommended practices to guide the development and maintenance of a high-quality, inclusive program. Checklists in both the guidebook and an accompanying workbook assist leaders with assessing the climate needed to sustain inclusion (e.g., Hemmeter & Smith, 2005). Smart leaders will seek NAEYC accreditation and use both NAEYC accreditation standards and DEC recommended practices to continuously improve program quality and practice.

Smart leaders will seek NAEYC accreditation and use both NAEYC accreditation standards and DEC recommended practices to continuously improve program quality and practice.

STAFF AND FAMILY CONSIDERATIONS

Driving back to her program, Nan reflects on her colleagues' advice. A smart first step, she thinks, will be to seek NAEYC accreditation. This will not only ensure that those outside of her program—parents, families, teachers, and other programs—will recognize hers as a high-quality early childhood setting but also help her ensure that her program and staff consistently and continuously guide child learning safely and appropriately. She could also begin to take a closer look at the practices she and her staff are using. She suspects her staff are respectful but that they, like her, lack the knowledge and specialized skill set to effectively and

FYI 4.4

Quality Rating Improvement Systems: Rating Program Quality and Capacity

What Is It?

QRIS is a continuous quality improvement effort, the aim of which is "to improve the quality of early and school-age care and education programs through the alignment and coordination of system-wide initiatives" (National Center on Child Care Quality Improvement [NCCCQI], 2011, p. 1). States coordinate multiple standards for early learning, quality improvement initiatives, and professional development efforts into one entity that will systematically "assess, improve, and communicate the level of [early childhood program] quality" to the broader community (NCCCQI, 2011; Office of Child Care, 2012, p. 1).

How Does It Work?

Early childhood programs are rated according to their ability to meet defined features, similar to how a travel web site might rate and rank hotels for travelers. Programs are rated according to several features, including "1) standards, 2) accountability measures, 3) program and practitioner outreach and support, 4) financial incentives, and 5) parent/consumer education efforts" (Office of Child Care, 2012, p. 1). The rating system allows families to differentiate high-quality programs from those of lesser or poor quality.

What Drives It?

Other than the need for an effort to "elevate program quality and capacity," a desire to coordinate multiple efforts across a state or community that strive to support young children and their families propels it (Smith, Robbins, Stagman, & Kreader, 2012, p. 1).

How Is It Relevant to My Program?

Programs that meet QRIS standards demonstrate a level of quality likely to yield favorable outcomes in children. This means that the program is likely to score a higher rating, be chosen by families, and experience increased enrollment.

(continued)

FYI 4.4 (*continued*)

Quality Rating Improvement Systems: Rating Program Quality and Capacity

They are also likely connected to local quality and educational initiatives within the community or state, which may assist the program with meeting key elements needed to seek licensure or accreditation. States, in turn, are likely to recognize the program and offer resources to continue high-quality efforts. Finally, programs with evidence of improved child outcomes may also be able to lobby for additional funds from local school boards, business leaders, and other financing entities in the community.

What Can I Do to Get Involved?

The QRIS movement is gaining momentum across the country; however, not all states have a QRIS in place. To determine if your state has a QRIS or a QRIS contact, visit http://qrisnetwork.org.

individually support children with special needs. Considering this, how receptive will her staff be to inclusion? Is it important that they be on board? Or can she simply move forward with these large-scale efforts, insisting they are important to the program's future and success? She thinks back to an excerpt from a course reading: "A single agency, program, or provider often cannot meet the diverse needs of young children with disabilities and their families" (Harbin & Salisbury, 2005, p. 165).

Although inclusion is likely to be received well when introduced by an administrator or program leader (Lieber et al., 2000), it will not be enough to make it work. Although you may be driving the effort, you will be relying on staff and families to be champions for inclusion daily. In turn, staff and families will want guidance on how to make inclusion work and, more important, how they will be supported to make it a success. The next section reviews staff and family perceptions of inclusion, including concerns. Why note the concerns? Concerns indicate needs. When you understand the needs of both staff and families, you can develop a plan sensitive to their needs and embedded with relevant supports (e.g., time, resources) to facilitate continued communication and collaboration. We translate the research around staff and family needs next.

Although you may be driving the effort, you will be relying on staff and families to be champions for inclusion daily.

Staff Considerations

As you begin to think about how to build and operate an inclusive program, keep in mind that inclusion is likely to be a success when the following items have been addressed (Lieber et al., 1997):

1. Staff are involved in program development.
2. Staff share a philosophy for inclusion and instruction.
3. Staff share "ownership" for children's learning.
4. Staff communicate with one another, informally and formally.
5. Staff understand their roles in the context of delivering instruction in inclusive classrooms.
6. Staffing remains stable.
7. Staff receive administrative support and recognition.

For staff to "buy in" to inclusion, they will need to understand the rationale for it and know that support is available. Many individuals are involved in providing services to children with disabilities, including ECE classroom teachers, ECSE teachers, and specialists (e.g., occupational therapists) to name a few. In a qualitative study of four inclusive models across 16 early childhood programs nationwide, Lieber and colleagues (1997) found that teachers viewed inclusion favorably when they were part of the decision-making process. Observations and interviews revealed that teachers felt a sense of ownership when they were invited to participate in developing the program, when they were given time and resources to collaborate with each other and specialists to promote child learning (e.g., touching base about a child's needs during a routine planning time), and when administrative support was "available" (Lieber et al., 1997). Staff were less enthusiastic about inclusion when their or others' roles were not clearly delineated or when their philosophies about inclusion differed from those of other adults in the same setting. This led to confusion about how to support children, for example, within daily activities or outside the classroom. A common theme that emerged was the value of shared responsibility that led to a collegial investment in inclusion, suggesting that relationships between adults in inclusive settings matter and do influence inclusion's success across early childhood settings.

Teachers view inclusion favorably when they are part of the decision-making process.

Prior to the summer, Nan discussed with several staff members her interest in moving toward an inclusive model. This was based on several families approaching her, inquiring whether the program could support their children with developmental delays. It was just what Nan needed to make the case to her staff. Nan had a strong relationship with her staff, however, so she spoke with them informally, individually, as well as in small groups and learned that staff were indeed interested in including young children with special needs but that they needed more information and more training. Many were comfortable teaching a typical early childhood classroom but felt unsure about how to individualize instruction and activities for children with varying needs. This was where they would depend on her to provide guidance.

Two years ago, Nan decided to provide teachers with a coordinated planning time to encourage collaborative thinking and planning. She creatively arranged for teachers' aides and student interns to monitor each class during naptime, relieving teachers from these duties so that they could meet in teams or across teams to plan instruction and activities, to share ideas, and to think through any issues they were experiencing. One teaching team was having a particularly hard time with a child who was demonstrating challenging behaviors. This child was in his 2nd year in the program, so Nan encouraged his prior teachers to meet with his current teachers to talk about his behaviors and strategies they found helpful for managing them. On their own, these teachers set aside 2 days a week to meet, not only to talk about this particular child, but also to share activities they found helpful with preventing challenging behaviors and managing their classrooms more effectively. When Nan learned about this, she praised their ingenuity and asked them if they might consider presenting an in-service workshop to other staff about preventing and reducing challenging behaviors. These four teachers were thrilled and worked together to develop and lead an interactive workshop for all staff.

At the end of the year, several teachers expressed their appreciation for Nan's designated time to share ideas and plan with other teachers. The teaching staff not only felt supported by Nan as a director, but they also felt as if they were part of a larger team working together to support all children in the program as well as each other.

Reflecting on this feedback, Nan realized few staff had left the program since she initiated this practice. She wondered: Could she use this planning time as a springboard for the collaborative work needed to seek accreditation and support inclusion?

Inclusion requires considerable flexibility. Strategies or instructional approaches that work with one child may not work with another. Encouraging staff to communicate and collaborate is important and can provide a foundation from which staff can begin to develop clearly defined roles for this work. Questions about roles, such as the following, may arise:

- Will all teachers participate in planning curricula for the class?
- Will all teachers be required to collect data in the classroom, or is this the sole responsibility of the lead teacher or a specialist?
- If specialists collect data, should they schedule a meeting with the teacher to discuss observations and results?
- Who will be responsible for speaking to parents?

Inclusion requires considerable flexibility. Strategies or instructional approaches that work with one child may not work with another.

Consider providing multiple opportunities for staff to share and discuss their individual responsibilities and any concerns they may have. One way to begin is to invite staff to record their individual responsibilities in the classroom on a sheet of paper. Then ask them to work with their teams (e.g., coteachers, collaborating specialists) to note similar or differing responsibilities. When two or more individuals identify the same responsibilities, ask the team to reflect on whether they should continue with the same tasks or divide and conquer. For instance, if both teachers and the specialist are collecting data on one child with a disability, ask the team to discuss whether this is a good use of their time, whether the breadth of data is needed, and whether they can rotate this task. Also compare roles and responsibilities across teams. Then ask teams to share how they addressed similar or differing roles. By encouraging this reflection and discussion, you offer staff a safe forum in which they may review and reflect on their responsibilities. It also becomes a safe place to problem-solve. At the same time, you can offer your assistance so that they know you are available, consult with them on new ideas so that they feel invested in a collective effort, and reinforce specific collaborative efforts with recognition or incentives. Concurrently, staff will begin to establish their individual and collective identities and voices within the program and seek each other's help when questions or issues arise. They will be less likely to feel frustrated and alone and more apt to remain with the program. In fact, Lieber and colleagues (1997) found that a lack of familiarity with one another and turnover impeded the necessary relationship building in inclusive settings. Continuing to provide this time for reflection and discussion will enable the gradual building of the collaborative culture needed for inclusion. (See Chapter 6 for additional collaboration building strategies.)

Let us fast-forward to the fall. Based on feedback from teachers and on the knowledge that staff need time and resources to reflect on and improve practice to plan effective instruction, Nan maintained the coordinated planning time and used it as a starting point to initiate her inclusion efforts. She identified two priorities: NAEYC accreditation and establishing a programwide vision that reflects the program's commitment to inclusion.

Nan recognized that, as director, she was the leader of this effort, so she needed to guide and facilitate this work. She also realized that she was more likely to be successful if her staff were on board.

Because teachers expressed interest in inclusion at the conclusion of the previous year but admitted that they were not sure how to proceed, Nan decided to draft both a philosophy and mission of the school that addressed the inclusion of young children with special needs as well as a plan with a time line of how she saw this work progressing. The plan consisted of the following elements:

- *Continued planning time*

- *A teacher exchange opportunity to routinely observe and speak with teachers from a high-quality preschool in their district that successfully included children with special needs*
- *Some suggested fund-raising efforts to build their professional development funding pool*

She felt this starting point would provide teachers with the assurance that she had a clear goal—inclusion—and concrete steps to move the program closer to that goal. She presented this plan to teachers at their first meeting of the year and emphasized strongly that this plan was only possible if all were on board, all were committed, and all worked together. Because she too would be learning about inclusion and the larger special education system and field, she would be learning with her staff and relying on them to share their teaching expertise to refine the program philosophy and to improve the quality of the program and practices to support all young children. She, in turn, would begin to build relationships with neighboring programs, individuals, and organizations in the community to seek funding to sustain this work. As such, she began to model the process of establishing roles.

She also began to clarify expectations. She proposed setting aside 1 day a week to revisit and revise this plan as needed and to share progress as they all learned more. The remaining 4 days, she felt, should be reserved for teacher planning and meeting. She was honest and said that this work would be hard and would take time but that she was confident they could accomplish their goal if they worked together. Continuous and constructive communication would be important to move this effort forward, and she pledged to do her best to model and support this. She concluded the meeting by asking the team to review the plan, talk with one another, and to come up with questions for their next meeting. She also suggested that, if all were on board, it may be useful (and fun) to develop a title for this plan based on what was meaningful to them as enthusiastic and dedicated teachers of young children.

Family Considerations

The next Monday, staff met during the designated planning time to talk about Nan's plan and to share questions they had. Nan had encouraged staff to talk with each other about the plan, and they had done exactly that. One question that many teachers had was about family involvement. Could the teaching staff alone come up with an approach that would meet the needs of the families they were serving? One teacher suggested that families rely on teachers for their educational knowledge and expertise, so they would likely appreciate being involved but may not think they could contribute a great deal. Nan acknowledged this point and probed further—did everyone feel this way? Two other teachers jumped in, saying they did not yet have the expertise, so could families truly rely on them alone to develop a sound plan? Another teacher acknowledged this concern and suggested that this may be a good reason to include 1–2 family members of children with and without special needs so that they could understand what concerns families might have in this effort.

For this first meeting, Nan served as both facilitator and note-taker. She wanted to model these roles for staff but also facilitate a productive conversation that would lead to agreed-on actions. So she summarized and then probed further.

"It appears that we all want to be thoughtful in this approach, and this is good! We are investing our time and effort into this plan so we should be talking about our questions and considerations." She summarized teachers' points and offered a suggestion based on some initial research she conducted. She had already started the process of building relationships with other schools. One director was enthusiastic about the teacher exchange program Nan proposed. The program had learned many lessons that they would be happy to share. One of these lessons involved families. Interestingly, this program had similar conversations about whether to involve families but decided after thoughtful conversations that it was best to proceed with only program staff. Staff worked well together, collaboratively developed an inclusive mission, secured funding, and successfully received NAEYC accreditation. The program then began enrolling children with disabilities. Families of typically developing children became outraged. They did not understand the rationale for the change and argued that their children would likely lose skills as a result of teachers needing to spend more time with children with disabilities. They aired their concerns at a parent meeting, and many of the parents of children with disabilities felt disrespected. The director mentioned that it took a great deal of time to repair staff relationships with families and to rebuild a sense of trust among families. Looking back, the director would have included family members of children with and without disabilities. She also suggested pulling together some fact sheets showing the benefits of inclusion for all children. This would be useful not only for families but also for staff and could be used as a starting point to explore concerns at meetings. The director also mentioned that, when programs include families in the decision-making process, families are likely to feel that they have a voice in improving educational opportunities for their children.

They learn to work with staff, and staff, in turn, become more aware of the parent perspective. By engaging families, Nan's staff could anticipate questions families would have and proactively implement strategies that would educate parents about the value of inclusion for all their children.

In addition to considering the needs of your staff, you will also need to consider the needs of families with children with disabilities and those with typically developing children. Many will want to understand the rationale for inclusion. Inviting a parent to participate in the planning process along with staff will ensure that families are represented at the table (see Chapter 6) and that inclusion is defined in a way that makes sense to everyone (Schwartz, Sandall, Odom, Horn, & Beckman, 2002). This approach will be particularly powerful in community-based programs or Head Start programs that are often developed to meet the needs of families within a locale. Pause here to review DEC's recommended, family-based practices in Activity Corner 4.5. Also, if your program is private or faith based, in addition to families, you may also need to gain the support of the board of directors. Visit Quick Tips 4.2 for strategies. In addition, Resource Corner 4.1 offers strategies for Head Start programs.

Inviting a parent to participate in the planning process along with staff will ensure that families are represented at the table.

ACTIVITY CORNER 4.5
Division for Early Childhood Recommended Practices: Family-Based Practices

Review the DEC family-based practices strand for tips on how to assess the priorities of families in your community (Trivette & Dunst, 2005).

Other families may express concern about the amount of attention their child may receive—will children with disabilities receive more individualized attention, leaving typically developing children to spend time on their own?

QUICK TIPS 4.1

Challenges and Solutions

Solutions to potential challenges such as a negative parent reaction to inclusion may be found in Chapter 7.

Some other families will want information and reassurance. Will inclusion work? Do you have a plan in place? Is the program equipped to service the needs of culturally, linguistically, and ability-diverse children (Schwartz, Sandall, Odom, Horn, & Beckman, 2002)? Do all children truly benefit? For the latter question, refer to Chapter 3 for talking points. Your ability to answer these questions (and likely many more) will depend largely on your commitment to quality. Programs developed with NAEYC standards and DEC recommended practices in mind are likely to build in the supports that will lead to improved child behavior, learning, and development. Simply developing or sharing an "an eloquent philosophy, statement and elaborate organizational chart" will not assuage parent concerns (Schwartz, Sandall, Odom, Horn, & Beckman, 2002, p. 24). Families will want to know specifically how your program will provide those high-quality experiences that will promote each child's learning. Research has shown that early childhood programs that were successful at collaborating with parents had better outcomes for children with disabilities than programs that did not (Bronfenbrenner, 1979). Embrace families as key partners in your inclusion effort (see Chapter 6). Take note of any issues that arise with families. Review Quick Tips 4.1 and then visit Chapter 7 for suggestions on how to address them.

Embrace families as key partners in your inclusion effort.

Teachers expressed their appreciation for Nan's efforts to learn more about this process from another, more experienced program. As a result, staff unanimously decided that it would be best to include families in these planning meetings. Several teachers suggested family members they thought would serve as strong representatives.

As facilitator, Nan moved the group forward. She suggested they formally invite these family members to join their next meeting. One nice way to do this would be to prepare a letter on the program's letterhead. This letter would generally describe the program's interest in improving quality and practices to better serve all young children, and that to do this, it would be important to consider the family perspective. Teachers agreed that families would appreciate this special and unique invitation.

Nan also suggested that staff begin to think about concerns that families might have about inclusion. Not only would this show families that staff are considering family needs and priorities, but this also would allow her some time to conduct more research about the benefits of inclusion for all children. This way, Nan would come to the next meeting with concrete evidence that inclusion works and that the charge of this working group would be to figure out how to make it work given the unique culture of this program and its community.

QUICK TIPS 4.2

For Private Programs

Is your program private and/or faith based? If so, your program may be driven by a board of directors. Enlisting the support of board members, along with families, as key partners will also be important. Keep them apprised of efforts to assess program readiness and involve them as you would staff and families. Chapter 6 offers additional strategies to include board members in your inclusion leadership team (ILT).

FINAL THOUGHTS

As mentioned earlier, staff and families are likely to embrace inclusion when launched by an administrator or leader. Taking steps to ensure program readiness and to gain staff and family support will help you establish the high-quality program you will need to begin and sustain inclusion.

Nan was grateful for the opportunity to talk with her colleagues Mira and Suri about the progress she was making. She also thought it was important to continue meeting with other directors so that she too could ask questions, problem-solve, and share resources. Most of all, she was pleased with how much she was learning simply by talking with directors. She had not only developed a plan with their guidance and input but also begun to build relationships with individuals and programs in her community—this is how she located the neighboring program to begin her own teacher exchange to support her teachers! Meanwhile, as Mira and Suri progressed in their efforts, they continued to share lessons learned.

At the next meeting, it was Nan's turn to share progress. Nan had invited two families to participate in planning meetings, and both were honored that they were asked and agreed to join the effort. The family of a child with autism included a "traditional" family—a husband, a wife, a biological sibling, and several pets. This family spoke English as a second language. The family of a typical child was less "traditional"—with two dads and an adopted sibling. All family members spoke English as their first language, and the family lived in an affluent community.

At the beginning of the meeting, Nan introduced the purpose of the meeting and the proposed plan. She emphasized the importance of understanding family priorities, concerns, and needs—specifically around inclusion—and asked the families to share these with the teaching staff.

Interestingly, her staff had only thought about inclusion from an ability standpoint. Hearing from the less "traditional" family, staff realized that their mission should reflect their welcoming of all families. For example, this child called his parents "Papa" and "Daddy." On several occasions, teachers announced the arrival of "Daddy" and the child turned in anticipation only to see "Papa." This resulted in tremendous confusion for the child.

Hearing from the "traditional" family, the staff learned that this family lived in a less affluent neighborhood, depended on public funds to support their child's educational services, and spoke English as a second language. The language piece seemed particularly challenging for their child, who was diagnosed with autism, a disability characterized by delays in speech, communication, and repetitive behaviors. The child was hearing one language at home and another at school—should the parents reconcile this and, if so, how?

Would inclusion benefit these children?

Nan responded yes. She knew from her research that all children, regardless of ability, benefited. She was able to explain what these benefits were: positive social and cognitive gains in young children with disabilities, improved social skills, and greater sensitivity to individual differences in typically developing children. She was also able to explain that there is no research showing that any children lose skills in inclusive settings.

Both families and staff were delighted to hear this.

Nan thanked parents for sharing their perspectives and acknowledged that they brought up some critical points everyone should consider while moving this effort forward. Initially, as the staff thought about inclusion, they (Nan included) assumed that inclusion meant individualized instruction for children with disabilities. This meeting revealed to all that inclusion is, in fact, an approach, thus broadening their vision to welcome and include all families and young children needed to be the first step. This realization was so valuable and eye-opening to staff. Nan was sure that this was the first step in establishing a common philosophy toward a high-quality inclusive program.

Once they took the first step, they could strengthen the quality of their program via NAEYC accreditation and then improve the direct and indirect services needed to support all young children with special needs and their families. Just as Suri had said, NAEYC accreditation would help Nan create a strong, high-quality early childhood program. With this foundation, she could then refer to the DEC recommended practices to ensure the needs of children and families were met in culturally, linguistically, developmentally appropriate ways.

RESOURCE CORNER 4.1

For Head Start Programs

Planning for inclusion in your Head Start program? Visit the **Head Start Center for Inclusion** for practical guidance: http://depts.washington.edu/hscenter

Does your program already include preschoolers with disabilities? Review Sandall and Schwartz's (2008) *Building Blocks for Teaching Preschoolers with Special Needs Second Edition,* a guidebook for collaboration and the use of evidence-based teaching strategies to support individual child progress and learning in classroom settings.

REFERENCES

Beckman, P.J., Barnwell, D., Horn, E., Hanson, M.J., Gutierrez, S., & Lieber, J. (1998). Communities, families, and inclusion. *Early Childhood Research Quarterly, 13*(1), 125–150.

Bronfenbrenner, U. (1979). *The ecology of human development: Experiments by nature and design.* Cambridge, MA: Harvard University Press.

Diamond, K.E., Hong, S., & Baroody, A.E. (2007). Promoting young children's social competence in early childhood programs. In W.H. Brown, S.L. Odom, & S.R. McConnell (Eds.), *Social competence of young children: Risk, disability, & intervention* (pp. 165–184). Baltimore, MD: Paul H. Brookes Publishing Co.

Division for Early Childhood (n.d.). *Recommended practices.* Retrieved from http://www.dec-sped.org/About_DEC/Recommended_Practices

Harbin, G., & Salisbury, C. (2005). DEC recommended practices: Policies, procedures, and systems change. In S. Sandall, M.L. Hemmeter, B.J. Smith, & M.E. McLean (Eds.), *DEC recommended practices: A comprehensive guide for practical application in early intervention/early childhood special education* (pp. 165–188). Longmont, CO: Sopris West.

Hemmeter, M.L., Sandall, S., & Smith, B.J. (2005). Using the DEC Recommended Practices for program assessment and improvement. In S. Sandall, M.L. Hemmeter, B.J. Smith, & M.E. McLean (Eds.), *DEC recommended practices: A comprehensive guide for practical application in early intervention/early childhood special education* (pp. 243–263). Longmont, CO: Sopris West.

Hemmeter, M.L., & Smith, B.J. (2005). Checklists for family members and administrators. In S. Sandall, M.L. Hemmeter, B.J. Smith, & M.E. McLean (Eds.), *DEC recommended practices: A comprehensive guide for practical application in early intervention/early childhood special education* (pp. 265–280). Longmont, CO: Sopris West.

Lieber, J., Beckman, P.J., Hanson, M.J., Janko, S., Marquart, J.M., Horn, E., & Odom, S.L. (1997). The impact of changing roles on relationships between professionals in inclusive programs for young children. *Early Education and Development, 8*(1), 67–82. doi:10.1207/s15566935eed0801_6

Lieber, J., Hanson, M.J., Beckman, P.J., Odom, S.L., Sandall, S.R., Schwartz, I.S., Horn, E., & Wolery, R. (2000). Key influences on the initiation and implementation of inclusive preschool programs. *Exceptional Children, 67*(1), 83–98.

Lieber, J., Wolery, R.A., Horn, E., Tschantz, J., Beckman, P., & Hanson, M.J. (2002). Collaborative relationships among adults in inclusive preschool programs. In S.L. Odom (Ed.), *Widening the circle: Including children with disabilities in preschool programs* (pp. 81–97). New York, NY: Teachers College Press.

National Association for the Education of Young Children (NAEYC). (2008). *Overview of the NAEYC early childhood program standards.* Retrieved from http://www.naeyc.org/files/academy/file/OverviewStandards.pdf

National Association for the Education of Young Children (NAEYC). (n.d.-a). *Introduction to the NAEYC accreditation standards and criteria.* Retrieved from http://www.naeyc.org/academy/primary/standardsintro

National Association for the Education of Young Children (NAEYC). (n.d.-b). *NAEYC mission statement.* Retrieved from http://www.naeyc.org/files/academy/file/OverviewStandards.pdf

National Association for the Education of Young Children (NAEYC). (n.d.-c). *The 10 NAEYC program standards.* Retrieved from http://families.naeyc.org/accredited-article/10-naeyc-program-standards

National Center on Child Care Quality Improvement (NCCCQI). (2011, November). *QRIS resource guide.* Retrieved from https://occqrisguide.icfwebservices.com/files/QRIS%20Resource%20Guide_2011.pdf

Neisworth, J.T., & Bagnato, S.J. (2005). In S. Sandall, M.L. Hemmeter, B.J. Smith, & M.E. McLean (Eds.), *DEC recommended practices: A comprehensive guide for practical application in early intervention/early childhood special education* (pp. 45–70). Longmont, CO: Sopris West.

Odom, S L., Brown, W.H., Schwartz, I.S., Zercher, C., & Sandall, S.R. (2002). Classroom ecology and child participation. In S.L. Odom (Ed.), *Widening the circle: Including children with disabilities in preschool programs* (pp. 25–45). New York, NY: Teachers College Press.

Office of Child Care. (2012). *QRIS in statutes and regulations (No. 457).* National Center on Quality Child Care Improvement. Retrieved from http://www.qris

network.org/sites/all/files/resources/gscobb/2012-04-02%2011:56/Report.pdf

Sandall, S.R., McLean, M.E., Santos, R.M., & Smith, B.J. (2005). DEC's recommended practice: The context for change. In S. Sandall, M.L. Hemmeter, B.J. Smith, & M.E. McLean (Eds.), *DEC recommended practices: A comprehensive guide for practical application in early intervention/early childhood special education* (pp. 19–26). Longmont, CO: Sopris West.

Sandall, S.R., & Schwartz, I.S. (2008). *Building blocks for teaching preschoolers with special needs* (2nd ed.). Baltimore, MD: Paul H. Brookes Publishing Co.

Sandall, S., & Smith, B.J. (2005). An introduction to the DEC recommended practices. In S. Sandall, M.L. Hemmeter, B.J. Smith, & M.E. McLean (Eds.), *DEC recommended practices: A comprehensive guide for practical application in early intervention/early childhood special education* (pp. 11–18). Longmont, CO: Sopris West.

Schwartz, I.S., Sandall, S.R., Odom, S.L., Horn, E., & Beckman, P.J. (2002). "I know it when I see it": In search of a common definition of inclusion. In S.L. Odom (Ed.), *Widening the circle: Including children with disabilities in preschool programs* (pp. 10–24). New York, NY: Teachers College Press.

Smith, B.J., McLean, M.E., Sandall, S.R., Snyder, P., & Ramsey, A.B. (2005). DEC recommended practices: The procedures and evidence based used to establish them. In S. Sandall, M.L. Hemmeter, B.J. Smith, & M.E. McLean (Eds.), *DEC recommended practices: A comprehensive guide for practical application in early intervention/early childhood special education* (pp. 27–44). Longmont, CO: Sopris West.

Smith, S., Robbins, T., Stagman, S., Kreader, J. L. (2012, September). *Practices for promoting young children's learning in QRIS standards.* New York, NY: National Center for Children in Poverty, Columbia University Mailman School of Public Health. Retrieved from http://www.nccp.org/publications/pdf/text_1070.pdf

Trivette, C.M., & Dunst, C.L. (2005). DEC recommended practices: Family-based practices. In S. Sandall, M.L. Hemmeter, B.J. Smith, & M.E. McLean (Eds.), *DEC recommended practices: A comprehensive guide for practical application in early intervention/early childhood special education* (pp. 107–126). Longmont, CO: Sopris West.

CHAPTER 5

What Are My Program's Inclusion Requirements and Resources to Help Me Understand Them?

Sarika S. Gupta and Megan E. Vinh

We return again to Nan, our preschool director from Chapter 4, who wants to enroll children with disabilities into her private preschool program. As she moves through her initial efforts, she is suddenly struck with a thought: Is inclusion required in her private program? She remembered hearing from her colleague that Head Start programs are required to enroll children with disabilities and to specifically reserve 10% of slots for this purpose. Surely, private programs had requirements, but is it a certain percentage or simply a general policy? She also assumed additional resources were available to her, but where could she find them?

A variety of early childhood programs serve preschool-age children and their families. Though these programs share a collective aim of supporting young children, they may differ in their scope, meaning *how* they provide this support. In addition, unique eligibility requirements determine which children and families these programs aim to serve. The federal Head Start program, for instance, serves children whose families meet income requirements and children with disabilities (see Chapter 2).

As you consider your program's readiness for inclusion (see Chapter 4), it will be helpful to think about what your program requires regarding inclusion:

- What is the purpose of my program and what policies guide it?
- Is inclusion required in my program?
- What resources will help me understand inclusion in my program?

To answer these questions, you will need to know more about your program's purpose and its requirements. Returning to Head Start as an example, the program serves children with disabilities; however, its primary aim is to support child health and family self-sufficiency. This aim differs from the federal preschool special education program, authorized by IDEA Part B, Section 619 (see Chapter 2) and other programs serving preschool-age children described in this chapter.

Beyond each program's requirements, however, are additional federal laws that support inclusion across all early childhood programs, for example, the ADA (see Chapter 2). This means that administrators and leaders should understand not only what their programs require but also the broader federal policies that support inclusion nationwide. Fortunately, resources are available to help administrators and leaders understand inclusion across early learning programs. Knowing where this information exists and how to use it is just as important as knowing about each program's requirements.

> *Resources are available to help administrators and leaders understand inclusion across early learning programs. Knowing where this information exists and how to use it is just as important as knowing about each program's requirements.*

This chapter builds on Chapter 2's foundation of the federal laws and policies that govern inclusion by providing you with a deeper understanding of inclusion within each early learning program serving preschool children and their families. It begins with an overview of the types of early learning programs that serve preschool-age children. This chapter uses the all-encompassing term *early learning programs* to describe programs that serve children ages 3–5 and their families. In addition to describing their aims, this chapter also describes each program's requirements related to children with disabilities. It then reviews two federal laws that support preschool inclusion broadly—Section 504 of the Rehabilitation Act of 1973 and the ADA—and offers a starting list of resources to help you understand these laws and what they mean in your program. After reading this chapter, you will have knowledge of the following:

- The purpose of early learning programs serving preschool-age children
- The eligibility requirements for early learning programs serving preschool-age children
- Inclusion requirements in early learning programs that serve preschool-age children
- How Section 504 of the Rehabilitation Act of 1973 supports inclusion across early learning programs
- How the ADA supports inclusion across early learning programs
- Resources that support inclusion across early learning programs

EARLY LEARNING PROGRAMS AND REQUIREMENTS

Early care and education programs, also known as *early learning programs,* serve a variety of young children birth through age 5. Programs vary with respect to their intent, the population they serve, how they are funded, and other programmatic requirements (e.g., outcomes, curriculum). A program's purpose often dictates what population it serves and programmatic requirements, and funds are often allocated to support these aims.

Federal funding for early learning programs overall has increased tremendously over the last decade. The latest published spending amounts suggest that funding reached $20 billion in 2011, up 15% from $17 billion in 2000 (Barnett & Hustedt, 2011). Much of this funding flows from the U.S. Department of Education and the U.S. Department of Health and Human Services to states and regions across the country. This section describes several early learning programs that serve preschool-age children that are supported by funds from these two federal agencies. It also describes the purpose and eligibility requirements for six programs: Head Start, child care (funded by the Child Care Development Fund), Temporary Assistance for Needy Families, Title I preschool programs, preschool special education, and state-funded prekindergarten programs. Also described are general requirements for privately owned and operated preschool programs, such as Nan's.

Federal funding for early learning programs has increased tremendously over the last decade.

U.S. Health and Human Services Programs

The U.S. Department of Health and Human Services, or DHHS, supports eligible preschool-age children and their families through the Head Start program and the Child Care Development Fund (CCDF). The programs are listed in FYI 5.1 and described next.

Head Start Head Start is a comprehensive child development program that readies young children ages 3–5 for school by supporting their cognitive, social, and emotional skills (Office of Head Start, http://transition.acf.hhs.gov/programs/ohs). Initially

FYI 5.1
U.S. Department of Health and Human Services–Funded Early Learning Programs that Support Preschool-Age Children

- Head Start
- Child Care and Development Fund (CCDF)
- Temporary Assistance to Needy Families (TANF)

created in the 1960s, Head Start was designed to provide young children and their low-income families with comprehensive support aimed at "improving poor children's physical, cognitive, and social-emotional development; strengthening the bonds between the child and family, increasing a sense of dignity and self-worth within the child and child's family; and developing in both child and family 'a responsible attitude toward society'" (Rose, 2010, p. 21). The program works to offset the long-term risks of poverty by maintaining a focus on vulnerable populations—namely, those families living at or below the poverty line, migrant and seasonal families, tribal families, and other at-risk populations—wherever they live. Parents are recognized and celebrated as the child's first teachers and are encouraged in culturally and linguistically appropriate ways to improve their education and financial sustainability as a foundation to improve opportunities for their children.

Inclusion in Head Start. One unique feature of Head Start is its mandate to ensure that 10% of a program's enrollment is dedicated or reserved for children with disabilities (see Chapter 2, Head Start Act; 42 U.S.C. § 9801). Unlike many federal programs, Head Start disburses funds directly to local entities that then operate programs to meet community needs (ECLKC, 2012). Recent figures from KIDSCOUNT (2013) suggest that Head Start programs served 951,695[1] of 3- to 5-year-old children nationwide in 2012. Reflecting on the 10% enrollment policy, then, about 95,169 children served were likely children with disabilities. Currently, DHHS's Administration of Children and Families office manages Head Start.

[1] This sum is calculated from the number of 3-, 4-, and 5-year-olds served. See KIDSCOUNT (2013).

Head Start disburses funds directly to local entities that then operate programs to meet community needs.

Child Care and Development Fund Child Care and Development Fund (CCDF) is administered by the Administration of Children and Families and by the Office of Child Care (http://www.acf.hhs.gov/programs/occ/index.html). CCDF is authorized by the Child Care Development Block Grant Act, or Section 481 of the Social Security Act (Omnibus Budget Reconciliation Act [OBRA] of 1990, PL 101-508, 42 U.S.C. § 9858). In the federal fiscal year 2012, CCDF made $5.2 billion available to states to subsidize child care services for low-income families, including those living at or below the poverty line. The program aims to 1) assist low-income working families in finding affordable, high-quality child care and 2) promote program quality by strengthening the quality of child care options within states. Eligible children include those under the age of 13 "whose family income does not exceed 85 percent of the State median income for a family of the same size" and whose parents are enrolled in an educational or training program (42 U.S.C. § 9858, Section 658[P]).

States support subsidized child care for families of eligible children in two ways: 1) through grants and contracts with child care providers and 2) by providing families of eligible children with vouchers that parents may use to enroll their children in a state- or locally qualified child care option that works best for them (Office of Child Care, 2012). In turn, parents are able to pursue education and training to build financial independence to move off and away from public assistance. In addition to supporting families, states are required to use a portion of CCDF funds to support program quality, though largely states use these funds to do the following:

- Ensure the health and safety of children
- Build quality rating and improvement systems
- Build professional development and work force initiatives (http://www.acf.hhs.gov/programs/occ/general/occ_brochure/3.htm)

In the federal fiscal year 2011, preliminary figures from the Office of Child Care (2013) suggested that more than 1.6 million children birth through age 12 are supported monthly by CCDF child care subsidies. About 39%[2] of these children are 3- to 5-year-olds (Office of Child Care, 2013).

[2] This percentage sum is calculated from the number of 3-, 4-, and 5-year-olds served. See Office of Child Care (2013), Table 9.

Inclusion in child care. Unlike Head Start requirements, CCDF does not require its programs to enroll a percentage of children with disabilities; however, "states must give priority to children with special needs" as well as children from very low-income families. Interestingly, it is up to states to develop a definition for "special needs" and "very low-income." It is also up to states to determine what populations overall to prioritize. Theoretically, states could focus the use of CCDF funds to support the inclusion of children with disabilities if their definition of special needs includes those children who are eligible for early intervention and preschool special education services (see Chapter 2 and the next section; see also http://www.acf.hhs.gov/programs/ccb/ccdf/ccdf06_07desc.htm). States could also narrow their definition of *special needs* to exclude children with disabilities, leaving fewer settings in which children with disabilities may be included with their typically developing peers during the preschool years. The term *disability* is defined by IDEA and specific eligibility requirements (see "Preschool Special Education" section). *Children with special needs* is a broader term that encompasses children needing additional or individualized support; children who speak English as a second language, children with challenging behaviors, children with injuries, or children with developmental delays who do not meet the criteria for disability under IDEA, along with children who are identified as eligible to receive IDEA services.

Temporary Assistance to Needy Families In addition to CCDF and Head Start, the Administration for Children and Families also administers TANF, a welfare program administered through block grants to states that help families in need become self-sufficient (see http://www.tanf.us/#). Eligibility requirements are based on several criteria including U.S. citizenship, families with children, and family income. Also, families may participate in the program for up to 60 months. Specifically, funds "are available to working families with incomes up to 85% [state median income] (CCDF) or who are needy as defined by the state" who have children from birth to 13 years old (Barnett & Hustedt, 2011, p. 6, Table 3). Several services are available to families, including child care.

Inclusion and TANF. TANF funds do not specify providing funds to support children with disabilities; however, TANF funds may be used to supplement the CCDF, which prioritizes children with special needs. Through this indirect route, states and programs could use TANF funds to support the inclusion of preschoolers with disabilities.

U.S. Department of Education

Several additional federal entitlement programs focus support toward preschool-age children, including Title I preschool programs, preschool special education (the informal name of the IDEA Part B-619 program), and state-funded prekindergarten programs.

Title I and Preschool Established in 1965, Title I of the Elementary and Secondary Education Act (ESEA) of 1965 (PL 89-10) provides schools with funding to support the educational needs of disadvantaged children (Matthews & Ewen, 2010). Learn some trivia about ESEA in FYI 5.2. Part A of Title I allocates funding to states for this purpose. States develop a "low-income" definition and then disburse funds to localities depending on the percentage of low-income students identified within the school-age population, meaning children in K–12 (Matthews & Ewen, 2010).

Localities may also choose to use Title I funds to support preschool. Described by the U.S. Department of Education (2012) and Matthews and Ewen (2010), Title I preschool is a program of educational services designed to support eligible young children's social-emotional, health, and cognitive outcomes beginning at birth and through the age at which children may begin public schooling, typically kindergarten or first grade. States may use some or all of the Title I funds to operate a school-operated preschool program, use some Title I funds to support a district-operated preschool program, or use Title I funds to coordinate funds with other preschool programs that support eligible children (U.S. Department of Education, 2012, p. 3). Children eligible for Title I preschool programs include those "in schools where 40% of children are in poverty or academically at-risk children in schools with lower percentages of children in poverty" (Barnett & Hustedt, 2011, p. 6, Table 3). In addition, "children who have participated in Head Start, Even Start, Early Reading First, or a Title I preschool program at any time over the past two years; homeless children; and children in institutions for neglected or delinquent children" are also eligible (Matthews & Ewen, 2010, p. 2).

Inclusion in Title I Preschool. Title I does not support inclusion directly; however, states may choose to use funds to support inclusion in Title I preschool programs. According to the Council for Exceptional Children (2012), children with disabilities are eligible to participate in Title I preschool programs just as their counterparts without disabilities are eligible.

As described earlier, the U.S. Department of Education uses formulas that examine state poverty estimates and education costs (see http://www2.ed.gov/programs/titleiparta/index.html) to disburse funds to states. States may use Title I funds to "support a broad range of early education programs and services, in addition to traditional K–12 programs" (Matthews & Ewen, 2010, p. 2), which means states can determine priorities for this funding. States may also develop their own definition of "at-risk" and measurement strategies to make this determination as long as they do not use income alone as the sole eligibility factor (Matthews & Ewen, 2010). The funds require states to develop a program of educational services at no cost to families that is designed to support children's academic achievement. This means that states could develop broad definitions of "at-risk" to include children with disabilities, and they could provide services to support children with disabilities included in Title I settings as long as Title I funding is used to supplement rather than replace services provided through other requirements, such as IDEA (Council for Exceptional Children, 2012).

FYI 5.2

Trivia about the Elementary and Secondary Education Act of 1965

ESEA was retitled as the No Child Left Behind Act, or NCLB, in 2001 (PL 107-110). It will likely be renamed ESEA in the highly anticipated reauthorization. Visit http://www.ed.gov/esea to learn more.

Preschool Special Education Preschool special education is funded through IDEA's Part B-619 program (see Chapter 2) and ensures special education, related, and supplementary services to eligible children with disabilities, ages 3–5. States may also choose to provide services to 2-year-old children who will turn 3 during the school year (IDEA, 20 U.S.C. § 1400, 619[a][2]).

IDEA funding is administered through the U.S. Office of Special Education Programs (OSEP), which disburses funds to states based on each state's population of children, ages 3–21 (IDEA, 20 U.S.C. § 1400, 618). Children must be found eligible for special education services through an evaluation process that includes referral and identification, assessment to determine eligibility based on specific disability categories, the development and implementation of an IEP that includes goals to support the child's educational needs, an annual review of the child's progress toward goals, and a reevaluation of the IEP every 3 years (Anderson, Chitwood, Hayden, & Takemoto, 2008). IDEA identifies 12 disability categories:

- Autism
- Deaf-blindness
- Emotional disturbance
- Hearing impairment
- Intellectual disability (formerly *mental retardation*)
- Multiple disabilities
- Orthopedic impairment
- Other health impairment
- Specific learning disability
- Speech or language impairment
- Traumatic brain injury
- Visual impairment

States determine eligibility guidelines that align with federal categories. States may also choose to use a 13th disability category—*developmental delay*—that acknowledges the need for global support in the early childhood years.

Each child who is eligible for special education services must have an IEP that describes the specific services and supports needed to support the child's educational needs in meeting appropriate and challenging educational expectations (Anderson et al., 2008; Bruder, 2010). The IEP is developed by a team of individuals that includes the child's parents, professionals who work with the child, and other key professionals who will support the child (NICHCY, 2013). The goal of the IEP is to "(1) to establish measurable annual goals for the child; and (2) to state the special education and related services and supplementary aids and services that the public agency will provide to, or on behalf of, the child" (NICHCY, 2010). The IEP includes several sections (NICHCY, 2013):

1. A statement of the child's *present levels of academic achievement and functional performance,* including how the child's disability affects his or her involvement and progress in the general education curriculum
2. A statement of measurable *annual goals,* including academic and functional goals
3. A description of how the *child's progress* toward meeting the annual goals will be measured and when periodic progress reports will be provided

4. A statement of the *special education and related services* and *supplementary aids and services* to be provided to the child or on behalf of the child

5. A statement of the *program modifications or supports for school personnel* that will help the child make gains toward annual goals, be involved and make progress in the general education curriculum, participate in extracurricular and other nonacademic activities, and be educated and participate with other children with disabilities and children without disabilities

6. An explanation of the *extent, if any, to which the child will not participate with nondisabled children* in the regular class and in extracurricular and nonacademic activities

7. A statement of any *individual accommodations* that are necessary to measure the academic achievement and functional performance of the child on state- and districtwide assessments

   Note: If the IEP team determines that the child should take an alternative assessment instead of a particular general state- or districtwide assessment of student achievement, the IEP must include a statement about why the child cannot participate in the required assessment and why the particular alternative assessment selected is appropriate for the child

9. The *projected date* for the beginning of the services and modifications as well as the anticipated *frequency, location, and duration* of those services and modifications

Each child who is eligible for special education services must have an IEP that describes the specific services and supports needed.

They key component of the IEP that relates to inclusion is #6, an explanation as to why the child will not participate in the regular setting with his or her typically developing peers, meaning why the child is not being included to the maximum extent appropriate. The next section describes the provision that guides this component of the IEP.

Preschool special education services and inclusion. Inclusion is promulgated by a provision in IDEA called the *LRE*. As described in Chapter 2, and by IDEA regulations, this provision requires IEP teams to include a child to the maximum extent appropriate with his or her typically developing peers. Also stated in IDEA regulations, "special classes, separate school, or the removal of children with disabilities from the regular education environment occurs only if the nature or severity of the disability is such that education in regular classes with the use of supplementary aids and services cannot be achieved satisfactorily" (34 C.F.R. § 300.114 [a][2][ii]). This means that any amount of time a child is not spending with his or her typically developing peers in a typical setting must be justified by the IEP team, which includes the parents, and must be within the IEP itself. Review Chapter 1, which describes how IEP teams consider the individual needs of a child together with a continuum of early childhood settings to promote the child's full participation with his or her typically developing peers and to the maximum extent appropriate, given the child's abilities needs. Quick Tips 5.1 suggests a review of Chapter 2 for IDEA key provisions discussed here, such as LRE and FAPE.

QUICK TIPS 5.1

Review Individuals with Disabilities Education Act Key Provisions

Review Chapter 2 for detailed information about IDEA Part B, Section 619 and key provisions: LRE, FAPE, and supplementary aids and services.

Any amount of time a child is not spending with his or her typically developing peers in a typical setting must be justified by the IEP team.

IDEA, then, specifically supports inclusion, and through the child's IEP, a legal document that describes how each eligible child with a disability will be supported in the general education setting and with his or her typically developing peers. There is no cost to the family for preschool special education services as a result of the IDEA Part B FAPE provision (see Chapter 2 for more about FAPE). In 2011, 745,349 children received preschool special education services (TA&D, 2012).

State-Funded Prekindergarten According to NIEER (Barnett, Carolan, Fitzgerald, & Squires, 2012), state preschool programs have the following characteristics:

- Are funded, controlled, and directed by states
- Serve 3- and 4-year-olds
- Focus on ECE, versus parent education or work support programs
- Take place in a group setting at least 2 days a week
- Are different from the state's child care programs and initiatives
- May include programs that supplement Head Start programs

NIEER collects information about state preschool programs annually. In their most recent *Preschool Yearbook,* NIEER researchers reported that 40 state programs directed $5.2 billion to state preschool programs, collectively serving more than 1.3 million 3- and 4-year-olds (Barnett et al., 2012).

Inclusion in state-funded prekindergarten. Unlike Head Start and preschool special education, state-funded programs are not guided by federal legislation and may not receive federal funds. As a result, states are free to design and implement their own programs, which means they can choose whether or not to include children with disabilities, if they do not receive public funding (see the ADA for inclusion requirements in any program receiving public funding). Consequently, wide variation in state-funded prekindergarten program enrollment, eligibility, operation, quality, staffing, services, and monitoring exists. Of the total 1,332,663 3- and 4-year olds enrolled in state-funded programs in 2012, about 33%, or 433,973, received special education services (Barnett et al., 2012). Visit Activity Corner 5.1 to learn more about the state-funded prekindergarten programs where you live.

Wide variation in state-funded prekindergarten program enrollment, eligibility, operation, quality, staffing, services, and monitoring exists.

Also, unlike the federal Head Start and preschool special education programs, families may need to pay tuition, unless they reside in states in which universal prekindergarten is available at no cost to eligible or all families (see Barnett et al., 2012, for individual state profiles of state-funded prekindergarten programs). Take a moment to reflect on and apply the information you have learned so far in Figure 5.1.

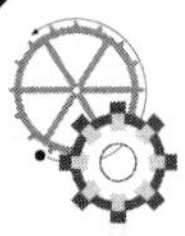

ACTIVITY CORNER 5.1

Visit the National Institute for Early Education Research Preschool Yearbook

http://nieer.org/sites/nieer/files/2011yearbook.pdf

1. Does your state operate a preschool program?
2. What are the eligibility requirements for the state program?
3. What percentage of 3- and 4-year-olds are served in your state program?
4. Does your local district operate a preschool program?
5. What are the eligibility requirements for the local program?
6. Do programs operate according to the calendar year, the academic year, or another cycle?
7. Do programs include children with disabilities?
8. Who is the main contact for the state preschool program?
9. Where can you learn more about the state preschool program (e.g., web site)?

Private Early Learning Programs

It is also likely that additional early learning programs are available in your community. Examples of these include private preschool programs, nursery schools, faith-based programs, preschool cooperatives, and family child care programs. What these programs share in common is that they are owned and operated privately by individuals, organizations, or corporations. This means they are *independent* in nature. They should, however, follow state standards for early learning. To learn more about your state's early learning standards, also called *early learning guidelines*, visit the Early Childhood Technical Assistance Center: http://ectacenter.org/topics/earlylearn/earlylearn.asp.

THINK, PAIR, SHARE

Select 2 children. Review the previous section. In the first column, note each program's eligibility requirements. In the second and third columns, record information about each child (or family) that may support his or her eligibility for each program.

	Eligibility requirements	Child 1	Child 2
Head Start			
Child care			
Title I preschool			
Preschool special education			
State-funded prekindergarten			

Figure 5.1. Think, pair, share.

Generally speaking, all private early learning programs should be state-licensed. State-licensed programs show evidence that they are providing safe learning environments that protect children's healthy development (NAEYC, 1997). Licensed programs also offer a basic assurance to parents and families that they "at a minimum, protect children by striving to prevent the risk and spread of disease, fire in buildings as well as other structural safety hazards, personal injury, child abuse or neglect, and developmental impairment" (NAEYC, 1997, p. 4). Given the importance of positive early interactions and environments on both short- and long-term development (Shonkoff & Phillips, 2000), it is important that all private preschool programs "protect children from harm, from threats not only to their immediate physical health and safety but also those of long-term developmental impairment" (NAEYC, 1997, p. 4). Incidentally, licensure is also needed to seek NAEYC accreditation, or national recognition that your program meets 10 high-quality standards shown to promote children's learning and development (see Chapter 4 for a detailed discussion of NAEYC accreditation and the 10 high-quality standards).

Inclusion in Private Programs Because private programs are independently owned and operated, they may design their own purpose and eligibility requirements consistent with their aims, which may or may not include children with disabilities. Learn more about the purpose and aims of your local private preschool programs by using the log in Figure 5.2.

Summary

As mentioned earlier, some preschool programs require the inclusion of children with disabilities, whereas others do not. Programs without such requirements, might assume, then, that they do not have to include children with disabilities. Two federal laws, however, suggest otherwise. The next section describes these two federal laws that support inclusion across *all* preschool programs.

Some preschool programs require the inclusion of children with disabilities, whereas others do not.

FEDERAL LAWS SUPPORTING INCLUSION IN EARLY LEARNING PROGRAMS

As we learned in Chapter 2, IDEA is the primary federal law that supports preschool inclusion through its natural environment and

PROGRAM LOG

Program name		
Contact information and web site		
Program purpose (e.g., mission)		
Age range welcome		
Includes children with disabilities?		
State licensed?		
National Association for the Education of Young Children accredited?		

Figure 5.2. Learn about local, private early learning programs. Develop a program log using this table.

LRE provisions. We also learned that the Improving Head Start for School Readiness Act of 2007 requires Head Start programs to enroll children with disabilities, further supporting inclusion.

Several additional federal laws broadly support inclusion in early learning programs, including Section 504 of the Rehabilitation Act of 1973 and the ADA. We revisit each act briefly in this section, focusing on how each supports preschool inclusion in early learning programs.

Section 504 of the Rehabilitation Act of 1973

Section 504 of the Rehabilitation Act of 1973 was developed to prevent discrimination of individuals with disabilities in programs that receive federal assistance (OCR, 2006a). Specifically, individuals—even preschoolers—with disabilities cannot be excluded or denied access to any program or activity supported by federal funding. Chapter 2 noted that "schools cannot deny a child with a disability the opportunity to participate or benefit from a service, provide a service that is not as effective as those provided to children with disabilities, or provide lower quality service." This means that early learning programs cannot deny children with disabilities the opportunity to participate, nor are they allowed to provide lower-quality, less effective services to children with disabilities.

Early learning programs cannot deny children with disabilities the opportunity to participate, nor are they allowed to provide lower-quality, less effective services to children with disabilities.

Americans with Disabilities Act of 1990

The ADA is also an antidiscrimination law that provides individuals with disabilities civil-rights protections across settings and environments (OCR, 2006b; see also http://www.ada.gov). It does this by guaranteeing equal opportunity for individuals with disabilities in 1) employment, 2) public accommodations, 3) transportation, 4) state and local government services, and 5) telecommunications (USDOJ, 2006). The area most relevant to preschool inclusion is public accommodations. *Private preschools, child care centers, Head Start programs, and even family-operated child care homes must consider accommodations for children with disabilities, including the following:*

- Aids and services (described in Chapter 2) must be provided to children so that they may participate.
- The physical structure of programs and classrooms should accommodate all children, and when they do not, appropriate alternatives must be provided, such as an alternate path of travel via a ramp for a child using a wheelchair.

Title II of the law ("State and Local Governments") protects children attending public settings, such as local programs or Head Start programs, whereas Title III ("Public Accommodations") protects children in private programs (Early Childhood Technical Assistance Center [ECTA], n.d.; see also http://www.ada.gov/2010_regs.htm).

Helpful Resources

Keeping track of these laws and requirements can be easy when you know where to learn more. For this reason, the following list gives several resources to help you understand how IDEA, Section 504, and the ADA have an impact on your early learning program. Use these resources to get started, and use the *Inclusion Resource Log* (Form 5.1; see Figure 5.3 for a filled-in example) to note additional resources you find or topics you want to explore as you learn more.

- The Center to Mobilize Early Childhood Knowledge (CONNECT). (2012). *Policy advisory: The law on inclusive education* (Rev. ed.). Chapel Hill: University of North Carolina, Frank Porter Graham (FPG) Child Development Institute, Author. Retrieved from http://community.fpg.unc.edu/sites/community.fpg.unc.edu/files/resources/Handout/CONNECT-Handout%201-4.pdf
- Early Childhood Technical Assistance Center (ECTA). (n.d.). *Resources for federal laws affecting preschool inclusion.* Retrieved from http://www.ectacenter.org/topics/inclusion/legis/fedlegisl.asp
- Education Law Center. (2010, February). *Pre-K policy brief series: Including children with disabilities in state pre-K programs.* Retrieved from http://www.edlawcenter.org/assets/files/pdfs/publications/PreKPolicyBrief_InclusionChildrenWithDisabilities.pdf
- National Association for the Deaf. (n.d.). *ADA obligations of private schools, classes, or programs.* Retrieved from http://www.nad.org/issues/education/other-opportunities/ada-obligations
- U.S. Department of Health and Human Services. (n.d.). *Frequently asked questions: Meeting the needs of TANF applicants and beneficiaries*

under federal civil rights laws. Retrieved from http://www.hhs.gov/ocr/civilrights/resources/specialtopics/tanf/faqtanf.html

- U.S. Department of Health and Human Services. (n.d.). *Summary of policy guidance: Prohibition against discrimination on the basis of disability in the administration of TANF.* Retrieved from http://www.hhs.gov/ocr/prohibition.html
- U.S. Department of Health and Human Services, Office of Civil Rights (OCR). (2006a, June). *Your rights under Section 504 of the Rehabilitation Act* [factsheet]. Retrieved from http://www.hhs.gov/ocr/civilrights/resources/factsheets
- U.S. Department of Health and Human Services, Office of Civil Rights (OCR). (2006b, June). *Your rights under the Americans with Disabilities Act* [factsheet]. Retrieved from http://www.hhs.gov/ocr/civilrights/resources/factsheets
- U.S. Department of Health and Human Services, Office of Civil Rights (OCR). (n.d.). *Know the rights that protect individuals with disabilities from discrimination* [factsheet]. Retrieved from http://www.hhs.gov/ocr/civilrights/resources/factsheets
- U.S. Department of Justice, Civil Rights Division, Disability Rights Section. (1997, October). *Commonly asked questions about child care centers and the Americans with Disabilities Act.* Retrieved from http://www.ada.gov/childq&a.htm
- Washington State Department of Health. (2009). *Child care and the Americans with Disabilities Act (ADA): Opportunities and resources for child care providers and families.* Retrieved from http://www.wrightslaw.com/advoc/articles/child.care.pdf

CONCLUDING THOUGHTS

Supporting the development of a high-quality inclusive program is manageable when you understand your program and its requirements and when you know where to find resources to understand requirements. This chapter provided an overview of early learning programs, their purpose, and whom they serve. It then reviewed two federal laws—Section 504 of the Rehabilitation Act of 1973 and the ADA—that collectively prevent the discrimination of children with disabilities from public and private preschool programs. It also provided resources that will help you understand more about the impact of these laws in early learning programs. We hope you use this chapter as a starting point to gather information about your program and before you begin the collaborative effort, described in Chapter 6, to initiate programwide inclusion.

INCLUSION RESOURCE LOG FOR MY PROGRAM

Use this to log to gather information about your early learning program and the requirements that influence inclusion in your program.

My program:

____

My program's requirements about inclusion:

____

The Americans with Disabilities Act in my program:

____
____
____
____

Section 504 in my program:

____
____
____
____
____
____
____

Resources to help me understand inclusion requirements:

____
____
____
____
____
____
____
____
____
____
____
____
____

Form 5.1. Inclusion Resource Log for My Program

INCLUSION RESOURCE LOG FOR MY PROGRAM

Use this to log to gather information about your early learning program and the requirements that influence inclusion in your program.

My program:

An independent preschool program that serves children ages 2 1/2–5.

My program's requirements about inclusion:

Our mission states that we welcome children of all abilities.

The Americans with Disabilities Act in my program:

Technically, because my program is not supported by public dollars (e.g., federal, state, or local funds), the ADA does not apply to us. That said, and given our inclusive program vision, we do invite children with disabilities into our program and encourage teachers and parents to work together to learn about and support each child's needs appropriately.

Section 504 in my program:

I'm not sure I understand what Section 504 means, other than it bars discrimination. But I do remember one director mentioning at our last districtwide meeting that one of her students who was not eligible for special education services has a 504 plan to support her educational needs in that program. The parents were thrilled because the child could continue to go to school with the peers she grew up with and because she received the individualized support she needed to support her developmental delays. I will make an effort to connect with that director at our next meeting.

Resources to help me understand inclusion requirements:

1. I want to review the requirements around inclusion, so I'm going to review this resource. I think I might also share this with my staff to reinforce their inclusive approach as they welcome students of varying abilities.
CONNECT: The Center to Mobilize Early Childhood Knowledge. (2012). Policy advisory: The law on inclusive education (Rev. ed.). Chapel Hill: University of North Carolina, Frank Porter Graham (FPG) Child Development Institute, Author. Retrieved from http://community.fpg.unc.edu/sites/community.fpg.unc.edu/files/resources/Handout/CONNECT-Handout%201-4.pdf
2. Even though we do not consider ourselves a "child care" program, I think it may be helpful to review this for potential resources we might use to better support families interested in including their children with disabilities in our program.
Washington State Department of Health. (2009). Child care and the Americans with Disabilities Act (ADA): Opportunities and resources for child care providers and families. Retrieved from http://www.wrightslaw.com/advoc/articles/child.care.pdf

Figure 5.3. Filled-in example of Form 5.1.

REFERENCES

Anderson, W., Chitwood, S., Hayden, D., & Takemoto, C. (2008). *Negotiating the special education maze: A guide for parents and teachers.* Bethesda, MD: Woodbine House.

Barnett, W.S., Carolan, M.E., Fitzgerald, J., & Squires, J.H. (2012). *The state of preschool 2012: State preschool yearbook.* New Brunswick, NJ: National Institute for Early Education Research, Rutgers University. Retrieved from http://nieer.org/sites/nieer/files/yearbook2012.pdf

Barnett, W.S., & Hustedt, J.T. (2011). *Policy brief: Improving public financing for early learning programs.* The National Institute for Early Education Research. Retrieved from http://nieer.org/resources/policybriefs/24.pdf

Bruder, M. (2010). Early childhood intervention: A promise to children and families for their future. *Exceptional Children, 76,* 339–355.

Council for Exceptional Children. (2012, April 20). *U.S. Department of Education issues guidance on use of Title I funding for preschool programs* [web log]. Retrieved from http://www.policyinsider.org/2012/04/us-department-of-education-issues-guidance-on-use-of-title-i-funding-for-preschool-programs.html

Early Childhood Technical Assistance Center (ECTA). (n.d.). *Resources for federal laws affecting preschool inclusion.* Retrieved from http://www.ectacenter.org/topics/inclusion/legis/fedlegisl.asp

Elementary and Secondary Education Act of 1965, PL 89-10, 20 U.S.C. §§ 241 *et seq.*

Gupta, S.S. (2011, January). *Policy brief: Strategies to facilitate and sustain the inclusion of young children with disabilities.* Denver: University of Colorado Denver, Pyramid Plus: The Colorado Center for Social and Emotional Competence and Inclusion. Retrieved from http://www.pyramidplus.org/policywork/advisory

Improving Head Start for School Readiness Act of 2007, PL 110-134, 42 U.S.C. §§ 9801 *et seq.*

Individuals with Disabilities Education Act (IDEA) Regulations, 34 C.F.R. §§ 300 *et seq.*

Individuals with Disabilities Education Improvement Act (IDEA) of 2004, PL 108-446, 20 U.S.C. §§ 1400 *et seq.*

KIDSCOUNT. (2013). *Head Start enrollment by age group* [factsheet]. Retrieved from http://datacenter.kidscount.org/data/tables/5938-head-start-enrollment-by-age-group

Matthews, H., & Ewen, D. (2010). *FAQ: Using Title I of ESEA for early education.* Washington, DC: Center for Law and Social Policy. Retrieved from http://www.clasp.org/admin/site/publications/files/titleifaq-1.pdf

National Association for the Education of Young Children (NAEYC). (1997). *Licensing and public regulation of early childhood programs: A position statement of the National Association for the Education of Young Children.* Retrieved from http://www.naeyc.org/positionstatements

National Dissemination Center for Children with Disabilities (NICHCY). (2010). *Contents of the IEP.* Retrieved from http://nichcy.org/schoolage/iep/iepcontents

National Dissemination Center for Children with Disabilities (NICHCY). (2013). *The short-and-sweet IEP overview.* Retrieved from http://nichcy.org/schoolage/iep/overview

No Child Left Behind Act of 2001, PL 107-110, 115 Stat. 1425, 20 U.S.C. §§ 6301 *et seq.*

Office of the Administration for Children and Families, Early Childhood Learning and Knowledge Center (ECLKC). (2012). *Head Start program facts: Fiscal year* [factsheet]. Retrieved from http://eclkc.ohs.acf.hhs.gov/hslc/mr/factsheets

Office of Child Care. (2012, March). *Child care and development fund* [factsheet]. Retrieved from http://www.acf.hhs.gov/sites/default/files/occ/ccdf_factsheet.pdf

Office of Child Care. (2013, May). *FY2011 CCDF tables (preliminary)* [factsheet]. Retrieved from http://www.acf.hhs.gov/programs/occ/resource/fy-2011-data-tables-preliminary

Omnibus Budget Reconciliation Act (OBRA) of 1990, PL 101-508, 42 U.S.C. §§ 1395cc *et seq.*

Rehabilitation Act of 1973, PL 93-112, Section 504, 34 C.F.R. §§ 104 *et seq.*

Rose, E. (2010). *The promise of preschool: From Head Start to universal pre-kindergarten.* New York, NY: Oxford University Press.

Shonkoff, J.P., & Phillips, D.A. (2000). *From neurons to neighborhoods: The science of early childhood development.* Washington, DC: National Academy Press.

Social Security Act of 1990, PL 101-508, 42 U.S.C. § 9858.

Technical Assistance and Dissemination Network (TA&D). (2012). *Data table: Part B child count 2011.* Retrieved from http://tadnet.public.tadnet.org/pages/712

U.S. Department of Education. (2012, October). *Serving preschool children through Title I: Part A of the Elementary and Secondary Education Act of 1965, as amended: Non-regulatory guidance.* Retrieved from http://www2.ed.gov/policy/elsec/guid/preschoolguidance2012.pdf

U.S. Department of Health and Human Services, Office of Civil Rights (OCR). (2006a, June). *Your rights under Section 504 of the Rehabilitation Act* [factsheet]. Retrieved from http://www.hhs.gov/ocr/civilrights/resources/factsheets

U.S. Department of Health and Human Services, Office of Civil Rights (OCR). (2006b, June). *Your rights under the Americans with Disabilities Act* [factsheet]. Retrieved from http://www.hhs.gov/ocr/civilrights/resources/factsheets

U.S. Department of Justice (USDOJ), Office of Civil Rights. (2006, April). *Americans with Disabilities Act.* Retrieved from http://www2.ed.gov/about/offices/list/ocr/docs/hq9805.html

CHAPTER 6

How Will I Support Key Program Changes?

Tools for Collaboration

Megan E. Vinh, Sarika S. Gupta, and Laura DiNardo

When children with disabilities are included in preschool programs, teamwork becomes a necessity.

—Lieber, Wolery, Horn, Tschantz, Beckman, and Hanson (2002)

Many young children with disabilities attend and receive special education services in a variety of early childhood programs, including Head Start, child care, and state-funded prekindergarten. These programs are tasked with finding ways to ensure inclusion for children with a variety of developmental needs and to provide children with disabilities with meaningful interactions with their typically developing peers (Rous & Smith, 2011). This will require considerable collaboration, both within and beyond a program. By *collaboration,* we mean exchanging understanding and expertise among team members (Rose & Smith, 1993) to build a

> shared commitment to inclusion, supportive policies and procedures in all agencies, and professional development opportunities across agencies so that personnel can work together and share expertise related to meeting the educational needs of all children. (Rous & Smith, 2011, p. 9)

Collaboration assumes teamwork and requires both team building and ongoing support of team members. In teams, individuals are given focused opportunities to share and debate perspectives and engage in effective decision making that will ultimately inform educational planning for a child and his or her family (McWilliam, 2005). Administrators should know how to build and support a positive team that can lead inclusion efforts. They should also know how to engage those individuals who have a stake in the program's day-to-day operation and success. These individuals are called *stakeholders* and may include family members, teachers, specialists (e.g., speech-language pathologists, occupational therapists), professional development providers, program administrators, and perhaps even policy makers. With these key people working together, inclusion is more likely to succeed.

Administrators should know how to build and support a positive team that can lead inclusion efforts. They should also know how to engage those individuals who have a stake in the program's day-to-day operation and success.

The previous chapters described inclusion, its benefits, and how to determine if your program is ready for inclusion. This chapter provides concrete strategies to continue inclusion efforts with the assistance of partners, recognizing that inclusion is not something that can be achieved by an individual. Collaboration and teamwork will be critical in supporting and sustaining the key program changes you will be making. The chapter begins, then, with a guide to engage members of your staff, families, and professionals outside of your program. You will want to be thoughtful and systematic in how you approach and work with these (likely busy!) partners, so the chapter presents steps for collaboration that will help you strategically build a shared commitment to inclusion. Because much of what you do in your program is influenced by what is happening in your larger community and state, it will be important to consider the "big picture"—namely, the state and community initiatives that address inclusion or encourage cross-program collaboration. This is also addressed in this chapter, along with strategies to share your work and build relationships beyond your program to sustain your inclusion efforts and bolster a larger commitment to inclusion in your community. Finally, the chapter offers next steps for implementation. After reading this chapter, you will know how to do the following:

- Assemble and lead an inclusion leadership team (ILT)
- Describe the value of collaboration and identify concrete steps to engage members of your staff, families, and other relevant professionals
- Begin to track your efforts to build interagency relationships beyond your network of programs to sustain your inclusion efforts

WHY COLLABORATE?

Research has shown that collaboration among professionals produces better outcomes for children in early childhood settings (McCormick, Noonan, & Heck, 1998). Two types of collaboration benefit inclusion: intra-agency and interagency. *Intra-agency collaboration* occurs *within* a program, generally among individuals on staff, and is needed to successfully include young children with disabilities in typical preschool settings and to sustain their inclusion (Lieber et al., 1997; Peck, Furman, & Helmstetter, 1993; Wolery & Odom, 2000). When professionals share a common philosophy, engage in joint planning and decision making, exhibit mutual respect for colleagues, participate in program development, share ownership for the success of children, communicate, understand their roles, maintain stable relationships—all with the support of an administrator (Donegan, Ostrosky, & Fowler, 1996; Lieber et al., 1997; Peck et al., 1993)—inclusion is more likely to be successful. Less likely to be successful are programs with professionals that hold differing views about recommended practices and instructional delivery for children with disabilities (Peck et al., 1993). Programs should establish a *culture of collaboration,* meaning purposeful opportunities to exchange and share understanding of what works in a respectful forum (Donegan et al., 1996; Fullan, 2001). This requires time.

Programs should establish a **culture of collaboration**, *meaning purposeful opportunities to exchange and share understanding of what works in a respectful forum.*

Collaboration between two programs, or *interagency collaboration,* is also important. For young children with disabilities enrolled in a variety of settings with unique requirements (e.g., Head Start, child care, Part B, Section 619), "[interagency collaboration] has been heralded as the way to find new solutions to complex problems" (Selden, Sowa, & Sandfort, 2006, p. 412). Cross-program collaboration enables the collective use and accounting of fiscal, expert, and time resources. When administrators are aware of resources beyond their program, they can use collaboration to support and enhance inclusion in their program (Hall, 2002; Oliver, 1990; Selden et al., 2006). This should also ultimately improve program quality and individual children's readiness for school (Selden et al., 2006). This chapter offers strategies to help build both intra- and interagency collaborative relationships.

PLANNING FOR COLLABORATION

Key ingredients for successful collaboration include the following:

- Time
- Trust
- Flexibility
- A shared goal and understanding
- Anticipation and management

Collaboration also requires you to become an adaptive leader. Effective leaders recognize the multiple perspectives that individuals and programs bring to the table. They anticipate and prevent potential conflicts through collaborative decision making (Johnson, Zorn, Tam, Lamontagne, & Johnson, 2003). What can you do? Anticipate that professionals will arrive with a fear of losing control, ownership, and/or resources in their classrooms and programs and prevent this fear by acknowledging individual and program priorities up front. Family members with typically developing children may also feel a sense of loss, believing their child may receive less teacher attention if a child with a disability is included in the classroom. Acknowledge their priorities and fears up front as well. Model this planning process for your staff and your partners (Smith & Bredekamp, 1998), and then continue with the steps outlined in FYI 6.1 and explained in the following section to build strong relationships and a shared vision that can sustain your collective efforts.

Effective leaders are ones that recognize the multiple perspectives that individuals and programs bring to the table.

FYI 6.1
Steps for Effective Collaboration

(*Source:* Hayden, Frederick, & Smith, 2003.)

Step 1: Build a team
Step 2: Commit, communicate, and meet
Step 3: Develop an action plan
Step 4: Measure progress
Step 5: Seek external support

STEPS FOR EFFECTIVE COLLABORATION

Step 1: Build an Inclusion Leadership Team

> When programs begin inclusion, it is vital for participants to take the initiative in fostering program activities. At [school name], team members met with the principal to suggest ways to facilitate inclusion . . . During the following school year, a leadership team consisting of three ECSE teachers, a prekindergarten teacher, and a motor specialist became facilitators of the large-group meetings. The leadership team developed the agenda for each meeting based on the

> interests of the other participants, recorded the events of the meeting, and communicated decisions of the team to the administration. The team wrote a report with recommendations for the principal about how inclusion could continue to grow at [school name]. (Lieber et al., 2002, p. 91)

Beginning the effort with a team is indeed a vital way to establish a collaborative commitment toward high-quality inclusion (Hayden et al., 2003). It provides interested individuals with an opportunity to join together to achieve a common goal, your goal: high-quality inclusion. The team as a collective also models those key ingredients for successful collaboration mentioned earlier. As the leader of this effort, you can initiate team building by appointing or inviting several members of your staff, family members, and other relevant professionals to join an ILT. Over time, the team will collaboratively develop a vision for inclusion, plan the implementation of the vision, and make decisions along the way. Development of an ILT will sustain inclusion beyond the initial planning phase (Fixsen, Naoom, Blase, Friedman, & Wallace, 2005).

Initiate team building by appointing or inviting several members of your staff, family members, and other relevant professionals to join an ILT.

Identify team members. The initial step is to identify appropriate team members who can work together to accomplish an agreed-on set of goals and objectives. Quick Tips 6.1 lists a number of individuals that may be helpful in leading this work. It is critical to include families in this team. Specifically, families help the team understand and consider their perspectives, their desires, and any individual or collective family needs. Research also indicates that early childhood programs that successfully collaborated with parents had better outcomes for children with disabilities than programs that were not effective in including parents in the process (Bronfenbrenner, 1974).

Early childhood programs that successfully collaborated with parents had better outcomes for children with disabilities than programs that were not effective in including parents.

QUICK TIPS 6.1
Potential Inclusion Leadership Team Members

- Families of children with and without disabilities
- School administrator or program director
- Special education coordinator
- Early childhood coordinator
- Provider (e.g., teacher, child care)
- ECSE teacher
- Early childhood mental health coordinator
- Related service professionals affiliated with your program (e.g., speech-language pathologist, occupational therapist, physical therapist)
- School psychologist
- Social worker
- Program business director
- Board member (private or faith-based programs)

Also, bringing together professionals and families with varying expertise, including those who may not be familiar with ECSE or inclusion, will be helpful in considering the educational and programmatic supports both children with disabilities and typically developing children will need daily in an inclusive classroom and program. Suggestions to build your ILT team are available in Activity Corner 6.1.

Individualized instruction will also be a priority in an inclusive classroom. For this reason, it will be important to bring to the table individuals who know about early childhood curricula and assessment, disabilities, IFSP and IEP development and implementation, and data collection. Your program's readiness for inclusion (see Chapter 4) may determine which individuals you invite or appoint to the team. For example, if you learn that you will be including children with visual impairments but do not have a visual specialist on staff, you might consider inviting one from the community. Regardless of who you bring together, it is helpful to keep membership to a manageable number of no more than 12 in order to encourage participation and promote individual accountability to the group (Daniels, 1986).

Bring to the table individuals who know about early childhood curricula and assessment, disabilities, IFSP and IEP development and implementation, and data collection.

ACTIVITY CORNER 6.1
Potential Inclusion Leadership Team Members

Think about individuals both within and across your program who could effectively represent the diverse perspectives of the suggested ILT members in Quick Tips 6.1. Then write names down next to each suggested member. As you move forward with your efforts and develop new relationships in the community, revisit and/or expand this list so that you ensure the inclusion of individuals that represent your program, the children and families you serve, and their needs.

As you select team members, keep in mind that "teams have life cycles that progress from infancy to maturity regardless of their purposes or the tasks they must perform" (Friend & Cook, 2013, p. 141). As team members work toward a common goal, they will learn about each other, and this typically happens through the process summarized in Figure 6.1 (Friend & Cook, 2013; Tuckman, 1965).

For a new team, in which members are learning about the purpose of the group, individuals are likely to begin in the *forming* phase, remaining polite but guarded and interacting formally with one another as they get to know each other and learn about the group's agenda (Hayden et al., 2003). As members identify a common goal and vision, they will likely also identify differing perspectives, moving into the *storming* phase (Hayden et al., 2003). Opposing views may arise between early childhood special educators and early childhood educators. Early childhood special educators may emphasize data collection to monitor child progress on IEPs. Early childhood educators may oppose daily structured data collection, suggesting that it interferes with child-directed learning. At times, the team may seem stuck; however, an effective leader (see "Planning for Collaboration" earlier in this chapter) will help the team organize multiple perspectives and priorities into an action plan that will drive the collective group's

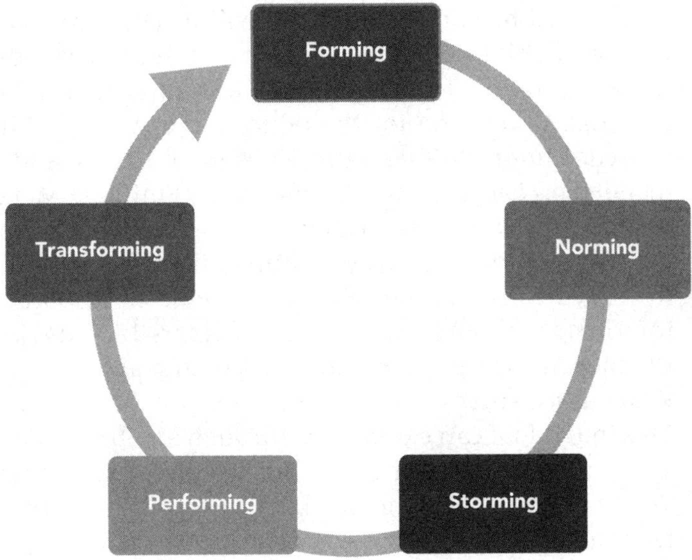

Figure 6.1. The life cycle of team development. (Sources: Friend & Cook, 2013; Hayden et al, 2003.)

cause, eventually moving the team into the *norming* phase (Hayden et al., 2003). The leader will encourage the team to provide feedback, address any competing issues, and discuss strategies to address these issues. The *performing* phase follows, as the team begins to implement their action plan. As the team continues, it will likely move back and forth through the stages, ideally building collegiality through strong leadership, or the team may *transform* to revisit the purpose, action plan, and even membership (Hayden et al., 2003).

An effective leader will help the team organize multiple perspectives and priorities into an action plan that will drive the collective group's cause.

Keep these stages in mind as you assemble your ILT. Consider the perspective of each team member you plan to invite and anticipate both the value and the challenges inherent in sharing differing opinions. For example, potential conflicts may both delay and inform this work. Referring back to the competing views of our early childhood special educator and our early childhood educator, the implications of including a structured data collection process into a program or classroom that does not typically collect data should be considered. How will teachers collect data to show improved child outcomes while managing a child-directed learning environment? Both practices are important, according to the National Association for the Education of Young Children (Copple & Bredekamp, 2009) and the Division for Early Childhood's recommended practices (Sandall, Hemmeter, Smith, & McLean, 2005). It will be the team's task to address these real-world considerations.

Continuing with this example, if inclusion is a new practice to the early childhood educator, it will be important to provide information about inclusion (see Chapters 1–2) and its benefits (see Chapter 3) as well as to consider inviting an additional individual who has led successful inclusion efforts to describe lessons learned. This individual can explain, or through an observation opportunity show, to team members how inclusion works (or will not work). The goal is to keep the work moving forward while keeping all team members informed and invested in the work.

The goal is to keep the work moving forward while keeping all team members informed and invested in the work.

As the work moves forward, turnover is always possible. For this reason, remember that, if new members are invited, you need to orient them to the purpose and overall process of this work. Linking the new individual with someone who has participated on the team is one way to approach this, keeping in mind that the team may revisit stages as they integrate a new individual into their collective efforts. In Quick Tips 6.2, we describe one way to engage your staff in learning more about inclusion.

QUICK TIPS 6.2
Engaging Staff

As the leader of this effort, start discussing your interest in inclusion with your staff. Invite staff members that are interested in and invested in inclusion as well as staff members who know less about it. Provide them with information about inclusion, the laws, and its benefits in an effort to share resources and build relationships. Review Section I for tips and resources.

Another intended goal of team building is to build relationships. The initial point of contact or conversation with a potential team member is an important one. Extending an invitation in person or over the phone adds a personal touch. Use the initial conversation to talk about your inclusion views and your proposed approach as well as to begin building rapport. You should certainly describe a broad overview of the purpose and focus of the ILT with the understanding that this will be further refined once the group meets. Strain, McGee, and Kohler (2001) suggest that "it is ideal if teachers can be selected on a voluntary basis. Often the first to volunteer are the most experienced and successful teachers who are excited at the prospect of a new challenge" (p. 355). When you cannot invite participants in person or by phone, consider sending prospective members a formal invitation, drafted in Figure 6.2. Figure 6.3 includes a sample RSVP and individual profile for members to complete prior to the meeting (see Form 6.1; see Figure 6.4 for a filled-in form). Form 6.2 (filled-in form shown in Figure 6.5) illustrates another way to learn about team members employed outside your program in order to share information about their services and resources and how they might benefit your efforts.

Set aside time to review individual and program profiles in advance of the meeting to get a sense of individuals' knowledge of inclusion, as well as community resources and programs that may support your efforts. Now that a team is in place, it is time to meet and begin the work.

Step 2: Meet, Communicate, and Commit

Preparing for the initial meeting. The initial meeting is your opportunity to build the rapport and trust needed to help members to feel like a team and to establish a shared vision. Knowing that this process will take time, it is important to set a positive and productive tone from the start and to get all team members "on the same page" by identifying a shared goal across members' work and interests (Hayden et al., 2003).

Prepare for the initial meeting by developing a meeting agenda, proposed roles for team members, and a plan to establish ground rules for how the team should work together to accomplish its goals. Also, review the roles of the individuals invited. It might be helpful to include with the agenda a description of members' current work positions and contact information. This approach is useful to learn more about each staff member's unique or shared roles and responsibilities, even if all members are within one program. Use Figure 6.6 to help you develop the first meeting agenda (adapted from Hayden et al., 2003).

Sample Letter Inviting Prospective Team Members to Join the Inclusion Leadership Team Meeting

TO:
FROM:
DATE:
RE: Initial and organizational meeting for instructional leadership team

I appreciate your interest in forming an Instructional Leadership Team and your willingness to attend our meeting. Our purpose will be to look at ways in which we can work together to include children with special needs and disabilities into our preschool program. We also plan to address how inclusion will benefit all children in the program, their families, our community, and our own programs and agencies. Our meeting will be held:

Date/time: ____________________

Location: ____________________

To help us prepare for this meeting, I am enclosing the following:

1. A meeting agenda
2. A tentative list of collaborative team members
3. An RSVP form (please complete and return prior to the meeting)
4. An individual or program profile form (please send with RSVP)
5. Directions to the meeting site

Feel free to call me with questions at _____-_____-_____.

I look forward to seeing you at our meeting.

Sincerely,

____

Figure 6.2. Sample letter. (From Hayden, P., Frederick, L., & Smith, B.J. [2003]. *A road map for facilitating collaborative teams* [p. 14]. Longmont, CO: Sopris West; adapted by permission.)

RSVP for Inclusion Leadership Team Meeting

Please return this RSVP by __________ (date)

Confirmation of participation

Name: ____

Program/agency: ____________________________________

Address: ____

____

Phone: _____-_____-_____ Fax: _____-_____-_____ E-mail: ________________________

____ Yes, I will attend this meeting.

____ No, I will not be able to attend, but I am interested in being a member of the team and wish to be invited to the next meeting.

____ No, I am not interested in being a member of the team at this time.

Comments: ____

____

____

____

____

____

Figure 6.3. Sample RSVP. (From Hayden, P., Frederick, L., & Smith, B.J. [2003]. *A road map for facilitating collaborative teams* [p. 15]. Longmont, CO: Sopris West; adapted by permission.)

INDIVIDUAL PROFILE

Purpose: To learn about our responsibilities, knowledge, interests, and abilities

Instructions: Provide information on your current role in the program, what you know about inclusion, as well as any questions you might have about inclusion. Finally, note any abilities and strengths you have that might support this effort. Please keep responses brief.

Position: ______________________________

Primary responsibility: ______________________________
____

Age of children with which you work: ______________________________

What you know about inclusion:______________________________
____
____
____
____
____

Your questions about inclusion: ______________________________
____
____
____
____
____

Your strengths and abilities: ______________________________
____
____
____
____
____

Other comments: ______________________________
____
____
____
____
____

Form 6.1. Individual Profile (*Source:* Hayden, Frederick, & Smith, 2003.)

INDIVIDUAL PROFILE

Purpose: To learn about our responsibilities, knowledge, interests, and abilities

Instructions: Provide information on your current role in the program, what you know about inclusion, as well as any questions you might about inclusion. Finally, note any abilities and strengths you have that might support this effort. Please keep responses brief.

Position: *Head Start teacher*

Primary responsibility: *Implementing a high-quality and developmentally appropriate early childhood program for young children*

Age of children with which you work: *4 years old*

What you know about inclusion:
I know a little about inclusion. I am a 1st-year teacher who has little experience with children with disabilities. Currently, I do not have any children in my classroom with disabilities. However, I know there are two children with disabilities transitioning to my 4-year-old class next year.

Your questions about inclusion: *What are recommended practices for including children with disabilities in my daily routines and activities?*

How do I emphasize understanding and social-emotional competence with all my students to ensure that children with disabilities are fully participating in my classroom?

Your strengths and abilities: *My greatest strength is my patience and humor. I am also very good at adapting my activities based on children's strengths and interests. I think this will help me when adapting curriculum for children with disabilities.*

Other comments:

Figure 6.4. Filled-in example of Form 6.1. (*Source:* Hayden, Frederick, & Smith, 2003.)

PROGRAM PROFILE

Purpose: To learn about the programs and services in our community and to use this information for planning purposes

Instructions: Provide information on services relevant to the education and care of young children, including children with and without disabilities. Please keep responses brief to a basic, reader-friendly description of what you do. If you have multiple resources/programs, complete this profile for each, copying this form as needed.

Program/agency name: ______________________________

Eligible population (e.g., age, income, special needs): ______________________________
____

Services: ______________________________
____
____
____
____
____

Number of children enrolled: ___

Number of staff: ___

Service location(s): ______________________________
____

Funding mechanism(s): ______________________________

How families access services: ______________________________
____
____

Parent fees (if any): ______________________________

Potential inclusion topics: ______________________________
____
____

Contact person: ______________________________

Other comments: ______________________________

Form 6.2. Program Profile

From Hayden, P., Frederick, L., & Smith, B.J. (2003). *A road map for facilitating collaborative teams* [p. 40]. Longmont, CO: Sopris West; adapted by permission.

PROGRAM PROFILE

Purpose: To learn about the programs and services in our community and to use this information for planning purposes

Instructions: Provide information on services relevant to the education and care of young children, including children with and without disabilities. Please keep responses brief to a basic, reader-friendly description of what you do. If you have multiple resources/programs, complete this profile for each, copying this form as needed.

Program/agency name: *Preschool Special Education Program in Utopia School District*

Eligible population (e.g., age, income, special needs): *We serve all eligible children with disabilities between 3 and 5 years of age. There are no income requirements.*

Services: *We provide special education and related services, including speech-language pathology and audiology services, interpreting services, psychological services, physical and occupational therapy, recreation, early identification and assessment of disabilities in children, counseling services, including rehabilitation services, orientation and mobility services, and medical services for diagnostic or evaluation services. We also provide school health services, school nurse services, social work services in schools, and parent counseling and training.*

Number of children enrolled: *15*

Number of staff: *5*

Service location(s): *We have children served in a variety of locations, including Head Start classrooms, kindergarten classes, child care, and preschool special education classrooms.*

Funding mechanism(s): *Federal and state funding*

How families access services: *Families, pediatricians, teachers, and others refer children to our office. We do a variety of child find activities to increase the likelihood that children with disabilities are referred to our office.*

Parent fees (if any): *None*

Potential inclusion topics: *How can we support inclusion when we have limited options for inclusion? Specifically, our state does not have a state-funded preschool program. We have one Head Start program in our district and one licensed child care program.*

Contact person: *Janice Smith*

Other comments: *None right now*

Figure 6.5. Filled-in example of Form 6.2. (From Hayden, P., Frederick, L., & Smith, B.J. [2003]. *A road map for facilitating collaborative teams* [p. 40]. Longmont, CO: Sopris West; adapted by permission.)

Inclusion Leadership Team Meeting Agenda

Date/time: ______________________________

Location: _______________________________

What to Bring

1. This agenda

Meeting purposes. The team will

1. Meet individuals within (and beyond) the program interested in inclusion
2. Identify strengths, weaknesses, opportunities, and threats posed by inclusion
3. Develop and confirm a team focus
4. Draft team ground rules, including a meeting schedule and membership
5. Develop a plan for next steps

Agenda

8:30 Welcome, introductions, and agenda—team convener(s)

8:45 Learn about one other: Review individual and/or program profiles and Q&A

10:00 Break

10:15 Assess program strengths, weaknesses, opportunities, and threats (SWOT)

10:45 Confirm team focus based on profiles and SWOTs

Based on what we discuss, what particular topic(s) or focus should this team pursue to implement inclusion in our program? Topics/foci should aim to benefit children and their families, the team members, represented programs, and the larger community.

11:15 Establish ground rules and confirm team contact list

12:00 Next steps: Follow up after this meeting and plan for next meeting

12:15 Evaluate: Team discusses why meeting was/was not effective and how to improve

12:30 Adjourn

Figure 6.6. Inclusion leadership team meeting agenda. (From Hayden, P., Frederick, L., & Smith, B.J. [2003]. *A road map for facilitating collaborative teams* [p. 17]. Longmont, CO: Sopris West; adapted by permission.)

Prepare for the initial meeting by developing a meeting agenda, proposed roles for team members, and a plan to establish ground rules for how the team should work together to accomplish its goals.

It is often useful to kick off the meeting with an icebreaker that builds relationships, sets a positive tone, and is grounded in the purpose of the meeting. Sample icebreakers are provided in Quick Tips 6.3 as well as more targeted activities that allow members to identify their personal interests and perspectives about inclusion. For numbers 3 and 4, consider organizing the team into smaller groups to promote rapport and to allow for detailed discussion. Then reconvene the team to encourage idea sharing related to the meeting purpose.

Beginning the collaborative process with an opportunity to share individual and program priorities is a way to determine a starting point for future action. These icebreakers not only provide a fun and meaningful way to build relationships but also provide participants with purposeful opportunities to communicate openly and share diverse perspectives (Johnson et al., 2003). In turn, participants will learn to listen to and acknowledge one another's feelings, encouraging a foundation for trust and confidence building, and eventually, a sense of commitment toward a shared goal that will be useful in tackling future challenges to produce successful outcomes (Fullan, 1993; Hayden et al., 2003; Smith & Bredekamp, 1998).

Following the icebreakers, transition the group to a discussion of SWOT (i.e., strengths, weakness, opportunities, threats) analysis, toward successful inclusion, and within a collaborative community (Hayden et al., 2003). Knowing what makes individuals feel hesitant or skeptical will help team members consider potential

QUICK TIPS 6.3
Icebreaker Ideas

1. *Five Fingers.* Pair off. Each person shares five facts (one for each finger) with his or her partner: thumb—your name; pointer finger—something you love to do; middle finger—someone you admire; ring finger—someone you love; pinkie—something you need to do more or less of. Reconvene as a group and have each pair introduce his or her partner to the team.
2. *Have You Ever?* Ask each participant to write a "Have you ever . . . ?" question on a note card related to collaboration or teaching. Model this with a personal example, such as "Have you ever had a child sneeze cereal into your hair during snack time?" Draw cards one at a time from a jar and whoever has had a similar experience will stand up, helping the group identify shared comical experiences in teaching and collaboration.

(continued)

QUICK TIPS 6.3 (*continued*)

Icebreaker Ideas

3. *Personal Schema Web.* Ask each participant to write his or her name in the center of a piece of paper, then draw three bubbles around it. Encourage participants to think about the parts of their lives that most influence their decision making (e.g., family, faith, education). Ask participants to share one influence and a specific example of how it shaped a decision they made in the classroom setting. Reconvene the group, and ask for several examples to highlight how individual perspectives are shaped by individual cultures and priorities.
4. *How Are We Feeling?* (An Initial Assessment). Set up four stations around the room (1, 2, 3, 4) and provide each participant with a piece of paper. Ask participants to rate their comfort level with inclusion on a number scale (e.g., 1 = completely unsure or uncomfortable, 2 = somewhat unsure but interested in learning more, 3 = interested and ready to move forward with guidance, 4 = ready for inclusion). Ask participants to crumple their papers into a ball and collect them in a bag. Then pass the bag around the room and ask each participant to draw a paper ball at random, read it aloud, and post it on chart paper or a white board according to its number category. You might save this list to encourage the group to identify questions or areas of discomfort after profile sharing and during the action planning phase (see Step 3: Develop an Action Plan).

challenges, both within the group and during implementation, and it will help you brainstorm strategies to mediate and manage the compromises likely to arise (Johnson et al., 2003). Through these initial sharing, reflection, and critical-thinking processes, you will see your team begin to develop a vision statement. Guide this process using the questions in Quick Tips 6.4.

Transition the group to a discussion of SWOT analysis.

QUICK TIPS 6.4
Guiding Questions to Develop a Shared Vision Statement

(*Source:* Hayden, Frederick, & Smith, 2003.)

1. Where do you want to see our inclusive program in 3–5 years?
2. What are the realistic services and procedures that will support inclusion in our program?
3. How will inclusion benefit our children and their families?

Record the vision statement in a place where everyone can see and refer back to it as you proceed through remaining activities. *It need not be perfect, but it should reflect team consensus.* Committing to and carrying out the shared vision is the next step.

Cultivating communication and commitment. It will take time and effort to cultivate commitment and open communication within your team to carry out the shared vision (Hayden et al., 2003), particularly if each member brings a wide range of knowledge and skills (Smith & Bredekamp, 1998). Two strategies to foster commitment and open communication include 1) discussing issues and differences so that each team member is aware of challenges that may occur and 2) keeping all partners "in the loop" to minimize miscommunication (Johnson et al., 2003). Additional strategies include providing time for collaboration and frequent opportunities to communicate and/or meet (Johnson et al., 2003; Wolery & Odom, 2000).

Time considerations. The amount of time needed for communication will vary based on the individuals involved. Assess the needs of the team, and propose a meeting schedule that will meet members' needs. Figure 6.7 provides a start-up schedule.

On a program level, a dedicated block of planning time for team members each week may work best. When team members include individuals beyond the program or in different agencies, a bimonthly meeting schedule may work better during the school year. Additional suggestions to determine meeting times and schedules are provided in Quick Tips 6.5.

Once the team agrees on a time, think about the goals for each meeting. Time is valuable, so these meetings should be thoughtfully planned with time to reflect, activities to support the shared vision, and opportunities to brainstorm. Team members will want to know

Figure 6.7. Prospective time line. This work cannot be completed overnight or even within a few weeks. Know that it will take time—likely months or as much as a year. Use this time line to guide collaboration efforts, and feel free to adapt it to your program and team members' priorities.

what to expect and will look forward to this meeting as a stable and safe space in which they can critically think and problem-solve, further reinforcing their collegial and driven teamwork (Johnson et al., 2003). You may also find it useful to note and then explicitly reinforce positive examples of collaboration that lead to positive outcomes on your team.

QUICK TIPS 6.5
Identifying a Common Meeting Time

(*Source:* Friend & Cook, 2013.)
Finding time to meet can be challenging due to scheduling and financial considerations. The suggestions here may help you think about when and how to convene your ILT.

- Schedule a back-to-back shared lunch and preparation period for program ILT members every other week, providing members with a focused 90-minute block of time to meet, discuss, and plan.
- Once a month, hire substitute teachers for ILT members so that they can attend daytime meetings.
- If funding is available, pay ILT members to spend 2 hours of planning outside the contract day. Hold members accountable for determining the time and submitting meeting notes.
- Think about existing professional development days. Set aside time in the schedule for ILT members to meet and work.
- Encourage ILT members to communicate from a distance, through e-mail, Google Talk, Skype, Adobe Connect, FaceTime, and other online platforms that will allow for the sharing of ideas and progress on assigned tasks.

Note and then explicitly reinforce positive examples of collaboration that lead to positive outcomes on your team.

Step 3: Develop an Action Plan

On to the next step—the *action plan,* the collaboratively developed document that will drive your team's work in the coming months (and possibly years!). Action plans consist of a series of concrete and team-developed steps to achieve the team's shared vision.

A written action plan, agreed on by all team members, enhances ownership and role clarity and reduces confusion. Furthermore, it may systematically guide team members to find common ground among individual priorities and agendas (Hayden et al., 2003; Johnson et al., 2003). We present one action planning form (Form 6.3) adapted from Hayden and colleagues (2003) with a filled-out example in Figure 6.8. Consider recording a plan in a way in which all team members can see it (e.g., PowerPoint slide, overhead projector, chart paper). Also, provide team members with individual copies of the form so that they can take notes on it during the discussion. Include columns to organize goals, tasks, relevant time lines, roles and responsibilities, and outcomes (Hayden et al., 2003). When team members can see what they are working on, how they will achieve it, what resources they will use, and what their targeted time frame is, they are more likely to feel empowered to drive this work forward.

A written action plan, agreed on by all team members, enhances ownership and role clarity as well as reduces confusion.

To facilitate the discussion, begin by restating the vision. Then follow the chart's structure from left to right and use the questions in Quick Tips 6.6 to guide your discussion.

QUICK TIPS 6.6

Guiding Questions for Action Planning

(*Source:* Hayden, Frederick, & Smith, 2003.)

1. What objectives and goals will support inclusion in this program?
2. What actions can we take to achieve these goals?
3. What resources will we need for these actions?
4. Who should be responsible for leading these actions?
5. Can we implement these actions individually or in small teams, or do we need to engage additional members with specific expertise?
6. What is a realistic time line for each action or activity?
7. What should the outcome for each activity be and how will we know when each has been accomplished?
8. How should we make changes to the action plan?

ACTION PLANNING FORM

Date: ______________________________

Inclusion leadership team vision for inclusion: ______________________________

____

____

____

Objective / goal	Action	Resources	People needed	Time line	Outcome
			(define roles)		

Form 6.3. Action Planning Form

From Hayden, P., Frederick, L., & Smith, B.J. (2003). *A road map for facilitating collaborative teams.* Longmont, CO: Sopris West; adapted by permission.

ACTION PLANNING FORM

Date: 11/6/13

Inclusion leadership team vision for inclusion: We are committed to increasing collaboration and leadership in our program so that the services we provide are seamless, inclusive of children with disabilities, and adequate in quantity and quality to meet the needs of ALL children ages birth through 5 years and their families.

Objective / goal	Action	Resources	People needed	Time line	Outcome
Develop and implement a collaborative personnel development plan to ensure that all staff and families involved in the process have the necessary skills to participate effectively.	• Self-assess the program to determine where staff and families are in terms of understanding of inclusion and developmentally appropriate practice. • Identify professional development opportunities in the community or online. • Identify continuing needs and implement professional development activities necessary to fill gaps.	• Preschool special education teacher • Staff that completed coaching training • Coteaching classrooms at the K–12 level within our district • Parent training partners	• Preschool special education teacher (facilitator of this group) • All staff • All families (if possible)	6 months	• All staff and families have completed the self-assessment. • All professional development opportunities already available are identified. • A plan for future professional development opportunities has been created and has begun being implemented.

Figure 6.8. Filled-in example of Form 6.3. (From Hayden, P., Frederick, L., & Smith, B.J. [2003]. *A road map for facilitating collaborative teams.* Longmont, CO: Sopris West; adapted by permission.)

Roles, Responsibilities, and Decisions As the leader, engage team members in writing clear goals and actions to establish realistic expectations for the group (see Hayden et al., 2003, for guidance). Provide examples and discuss each goal with the group to ensure everyone has a definitive and shared understanding. Through this discussion, team members may realize that they can actively work on specific goals, given their expertise, connections, or interest. At this point, ask team members to volunteer for actions they know they can carry out. To encourage team members' accountability to the shared vision and action plan, ask them to articulate their roles and their plans to the group. In order to reduce confusion, you might also facilitate a discussion to determine how decisions will be made once team members and small groups go off to tackle tasks (Hayden et al., 2003). The following vignette illustrates the importance of delineating roles, responsibilities, and decision-making processes within an action plan.

One team's goal is to include children with disabilities in their child care program. Through monthly team meetings, team members learn that funding is an issue. Team members identify "funding inclusion" as a goal. Fortunately, the team leader included the child care center's business director in monthly meetings. The business director, often tasked with searching for additional funding for the program, recognizes that this goal falls within her line of work, so she suggests taking on this responsibility. She suggests that she begin searching for state grant opportunities and initiatives that support preschool inclusion. The team asks her about a realistic time line for this work. The business director tells the team that grants and new initiatives are typically released in October, after the school year starts, so that schools have time to identify potential needs areas. Because it is August and too early to search for forthcoming grants, the business director suggests presenting a list of organizations she has sought funds from in the past at the September meeting. She will also reach out to other business directors in the meantime to learn how they fund inclusion in their programs. This will help her identify potential funding sources. At the October meeting, the business director will share a finalized list with the team and the feasibility of receiving funds from each organization (e.g., highly competitive). With team agreement, the business director can lead the development of a draft line-item budget that considers program needs. The business director agrees to prepare a detailed budget that the group will vote on at the November meeting. In this instance, the business director assumed the primary responsibility for a priority that fell within her scope of work. She suggested a realistic time line and a concrete plan with clear goals to bring information back to the team. With team input she can successfully draft a budget that considers necessary resources to support preschool inclusion in this program. Finally, with the team, she can finalize a budget for the program leader's approval.

Sharing this example with the team is one way to reinforce the importance of establishing roles, responsibilities, and the decision-making process. Consider also using the questions in Quick Tips 6.7 to guide this discussion.

QUICK TIPS 6.7

Guiding Questions to Establish and Clarify Roles

1. What crucial roles (e.g., meeting facilitator, specialist input) are needed to facilitate and sustain this work?
2. What are the responsibilities of each role?
3 Who on the team has the expertise to successfully carry out this role?
4. Would a team of individuals be more helpful or effective?
5. What is the decision-making authority of each individual or small group?

The Quick Tips 6.7 list will help the team examine roles within the group and during meetings. Returning to our earlier vignette, team members might suggest that they must all agree to any decision to pursue funding, hence the rationale for the final vote. At each meeting, they might revisit this role and decide that, for this action, it is a better use of time for the business director and the program administrator to make the final decision on where to apply because they might, for example, know the budgetary needs of the program, the implications of receiving specific grants, and how it might have an impact on program operation better than the teachers. Another example might be to develop a "parking lot" to store suggestions and comments that are not directly related to the meeting agenda for that day but may be relevant to future meetings or actions.

In addition to the action planning process, another way to document a team's efforts and decisions is to create an *inclusion team agreement.* An inclusion team agreement can be similar to other intra- or interagency agreements your program is implementing, such as a memorandum of understanding or a memorandum of agreement. The idea is to develop a document that reflects the commitments and decisions of the collaborative process (Hayden et al., 2003). It may be helpful to develop a fluid document, capable of evolving to reflect "the collaborative planning and problem solving" process that is more than simply a compliance tool (Hayden et al., 2003, p. 77).

Develop a document that reflects the commitments and decisions of the collaborative process.

You may already be familiar with interagency agreements because some state and federal laws require these to coordinate cross-program actions, such as transitioning children from early intervention (Part C) to preschool special education (Part B-619) or providing transportation for children who attend both state-funded prekindergarten programs and Head Start programs.

Step 4: Measure Progress

With an action plan in place, the team will accomplish much of the initial meeting's purpose. Before members adjourn to tackle their roles and responsibilities, it will be important to reflect once more on the team's efforts in this meeting. Allow time during each meeting (see Figure 6.6) for evaluation, an opportunity to revisit the team's commitment and measure team progress. You may wish to lead this as an informal or formal discussion. Questions to get you started are available in Quick Tips 6.8.

In addition, the team may choose to systematically evaluate each objective on the action plan to increase and improve the team's productivity and efficiency. This may call for the development of a formal evaluation plan, outlined in Quick Tips 6.9 (Hayden et al., 2003). The aim of this exercise is to encourage shared listening and to validate any concerns that might have arisen during the work.

As team members share concerns, note them for all to see. Then acknowledge and thank your team for sharing these concerns. Review these concerns at the beginning of the next meeting

QUICK TIPS 6.8

Questions to Guide the Evaluation Process

(*Source:* Hayden, Frederick, & Smith, 2003.)

1. What was successful about this meeting?
2. What needs to be changed for the next meeting?
3. Are our priorities and goals still relevant?
4. Where are we in the action plan?
5. Are we moving along as planned?
6. Do we need to make changes to our action plan?
7. Is the collaboration working for all team members and agencies? If not, what needs to change?

QUICK TIPS 6.9

Questions to Develop an Evaluation Plan

(*Source:* Hayden, Frederick, & Smith, 2003.)

1. Who needs to know the results of the evaluation?
2. What data are needed to determine if an objective has been successfully met?
3. What measurements are available?
4. How or from where will data be gathered?
5. What is a realistic time line to collect these data?

to validate all team members' feelings, to refocus the group on effective and respectful collaboration strategies, and to perhaps create new directions for your collective work.

Step 5: Seek External Support

To maintain and sustain your inclusion efforts, it may be important to seek external support—namely, from community early care and education programs and agencies, family support services, parenting education groups, social-emotional development and mental health stakeholders, and health care partners. Why is this important? Community events can influence your program's day-to-day operations. For example, some private preschool programs may be able to initiate inclusion for a year, but poor enrollment may have an impact on the budget and lead to cuts, thereby reducing the number of teachers, or their salaries, in another year. The program may then move to decrease extraneous efforts, such as inclusion, and redirect funds to daily operation priorities (e.g., salaries). Chapter 5 informs us that, although preschool inclusion often costs the same or less than the cost of public preschool, it may be sidelined because it is a new initiative. Drawing on the support of an established external network of programs, then, can enable resource sharing or creative financing strategies to sustain your efforts despite budgetary issues.

Further, programs that are well connected to the community are likely to design inclusion efforts that align with community priorities. If the larger community is invested in inclusion, and they hear about any challenges in your program, they may be more likely to support your program's efforts. This sort of collaboration requires established relationships with individuals in the community. For this reason, think beyond your program. As you guide your staff to collaborate and drive the inclusion agenda using the previously mentioned steps, you, too, should do the same on a broader level. To connect to the community, consider the actions in Quick Tips 6.10, and then use Form 6.4 (filled-out example in Figure 6.9) to keep track of your individual efforts to reach out to leaders and programs.

Programs that are well connected to the community are likely to design inclusion efforts that align with community priorities.

QUICK TIPS 6.10

How to Build Relationships in the Community

- Join the local early childhood council.
- Join another program's advisory board.
- Attend open public or private school board meetings.
- Individually contact early care and education administrators and leaders in your neighborhood and district.
- Join the local chapter of the National Association for the Education of Young Children or the state Division for Early Childhood.

RELATIONSHIP TRACKER

Name				
Program				
Position				
Inclusive?				
Where we met				
Contact info				
Next meeting				

Form 6.4. Relationship Tracker

RELATIONSHIP TRACKER

Name	Sarah Smith			
Program	Utopia County Early Intervention			
Position	Utopia County Part C (Early Intervention) Coordinator			
Inclusive?	Provides services in a natural environment			
Where we met	NAEYC meeting			
Contact info	Sarah Smith 555-8789 Ssmith@utopia.gov			
Next meeting	Will see at the next Utopia Early Childhood Council meeting			

Figure 6.9. Filled-in example of Form 6.4.

WHY WE COLLABORATE AND HOW TO ENCOURAGE IT

Simply put, we need to collaborate because there is strength in numbers. It is true that individuals are not always comfortable with collaboration. Even when collaboration is identified as an essential job function, preservice and other professional programs often inadequately prepare professionals to be members of collaborative teams. As a leader, however, you can consistently model and encourage effective collaboration, focusing on the shared goal of inclusion.

Coordinate opportunities for joint in-service trainings in your community and bring together professionals from different disciplines. Develop a theme based on inclusion that recognizes and validates the importance of each team member's background (Smith & Bredekamp, 1998). Lead the event with a keynote speaker who makes this connection and inspires action on behalf of all young children and their individual learning needs.

As you build relationships at the district, local, and state levels, invite individuals (e.g., business makers, policy makers) to organize events that inform the community about inclusion, the various agencies that can support this effort, and the multiple ways inclusion can be delivered (Miller & Stayton, 2005). Ground these events in the principles that guide professional preparation in the field. Competencies developed and set forth by professional organizations such as DEC of the Council for Exceptional Children and NAEYC are excellent starting points for this work (see Chapter 4).

As you move forward, also recognize that there are some inherent challenges related to bringing together a diverse group of individuals. For one, not everyone will always agree. Selden and colleagues (2006) found that interagency collaboration also had an impact on voluntary turnover in an organization they studied. They argued that this negative consequence emerged because collaboration can open "career doors" for professionals with high qualifications and experience (p. 421). As leaders, professionals, and even families learn more about and engage in interagency collaboration and pioneer inclusive programs in their schools and communities, they begin to establish themselves as experts in their field. With these credentials, said individuals may choose to pursue administrative roles or other career opportunities. As the leader of this inclusion effort, try to creatively develop incentives (e.g., leadership roles, staff recognition, supported registration or travel to conferences) within programs to attempt to alleviate some of this turnover. Overall, to address potential challenges, it is important to plan for collaboration (see earlier), to insist on following the earlier-explained process outline, and to remind your ILT that inclusion produces positive outcomes for all involved (see Chapter 3).

To address potential challenges, it is important to plan for collaboration (see earlier), to insist on following the earlier-explained process outline, and to remind your ILT that inclusion produces positive outcomes for all involved.

THE BIG PICTURE: PUTTING IT ALL TOGETHER

Collaboration requires work, but it can lead to many positive outcomes for children and families, for your program, and for the community. At times it may simply seem easier to lead every event and complete tasks individually, but ideally, you want these efforts to carry on even when you are not available. It may help to remember that collaboration is a process rather than a meeting or an event. The push for inclusion will remain strong when multiple voices and perspectives are present at the table, so collaboration is a necessary and essential practice for any group to develop priorities for a change effort such as inclusion.

NEXT STEPS: IMPLEMENTING INCLUSION

The success of your ILT is likely to result in inclusion—in several years' time. But do not worry; you should expect it to take time if you want to implement it successfully. Implementation is not a one-time event; rather, it occurs over a 2- to 4-year period (Fixsen et al., 2005). Implementation takes several years because it usually involves changing the behaviors and practices of adults in your program, creating conditions and supports that facilitate programwide change, and creating processes to maintain and improve the changes to benefit all children (Blase et al., 2012). To accomplish these pieces, you will need to build program infrastructure and secure additional resources. Think about infrastructure as specific elements:

- Clear direction and expectations
- Administrative support
- Experienced and interested practitioners
- Planning time
- Space

- Professional development, perhaps around early childhood development or disabilities
- Resources to support planning and individualization, which may be a new practice
- Coaching, mentoring, and supervision
- A process to assess, monitor, and evaluate child progress

Do these elements seem familiar? Many align with the components described in Chapter 4 to support inclusion on a day-to-day basis. They can be addressed, for example, through NAEYC accreditation and the coached use of the DEC recommended practices.

As was mentioned in the introduction, the implementation of inclusion is beyond the scope of this book. Seeing the importance of and initiating processes to develop an inclusive program is the first step. Approaching implementation with the same thoughtfulness you did collaboration will be important. With an understanding of inclusion, specific characteristics of high-quality inclusive early childhood settings, and collaboration, we are confident you will initiate an inclusion effort that will succeed.

REFERENCES

Blase, K.A., Sims, B., Duda, M.A., Fixsen, D.L., Green, J., Dughman, R., & Mullins, J. (2012, October). *Building implementation capacity.* Presented at the Regional Resource Center Program (RRCP) Implementation Core Team Institute, Chapel Hill, NC.

Bronfenbrenner, U. (1974). Developmental research, public policy, and the ecology of childhood. *Child Development, 45,* 1–5.

Copple C., & Bredekamp, S. (2009). *Developmentally appropriate practice: Early childhood programs serving children from birth through age 8* (3rd ed.). Washington, DC: National Association for the Education of Young Children.

Daniels, W. (1986). *Group power I: A manager's guide to using task force meetings.* San Diego, CA: Pfeiffer & Company.

Donegan, M.M., Ostrosky, M.M., & Fowler, S.A. (1996). Children enrolled in multiple programs: Characteristics, supports, and barriers to teacher communication. *Journal of Early Intervention, 20,* 95–106. doi:10.1177/105381519602000201

Fixsen, D.L., Naoom, S.F., Blase, K.A., Friedman, R.M., & Wallace, F. (2005). *Implementation research: A synthesis of the literature.* Tampa, FL: University of South Florida, Louis de la Parte Florida Mental Health.

Friend, M., & Cook, L. (2013). *Interactions: Collaboration skills for school professionals.* Upper Saddle River, NJ: Pearson.

Fullan, M.G. (1993). The complexity of the change process. In M.G. Fullan (Ed.), *Change forces: Probing the depth of education reform* (pp. 19–41). Levittown, PA: Falmer Press.

Fullan, M.G. (2001). *Leading in a culture of change.* San Francisco, CA: Jossey Bass.

Hall, R.H. (2002). *Organization: Structure, processes, and outcomes* (8th ed.). Englewood Cliffs, NJ: Prentice Hall.

Hayden, P., Frederick, L., & Smith, B.J. (2003). *A road map for facilitating collaborative teams.* Longmont, CO: Sopris West.

Johnson, L.J., Zorn, D., Tam, B.K., Lamontagne, M., & Johnson, S.A. (2003). Stakeholders' views of factors that impact successful interagency collaboration. *Exceptional Children, 69,* 195–209.

Lieber, J., Beckman, P.J., Hanson, M.J., Janko, S., Marquart, J.M., Horn, E., & Odom, S.L. (1997). The impact of changing roles on relationships between professionals in inclusive programs for young children. *Early Education and Development, 8*(1), 67–82. doi:10.1207/s15566935eed0801_6

Lieber, J., Wolery, R.A., Horn, E., Tschantz, J., Beckman, P., & Hanson, M.J. (2002). Collaborative relationships among adults in inclusive preschool programs. In S.L. Odom (Ed.), *Widening the circle: Including children with disabilities in preschool programs* (pp. 81–97). New York, NY: Teachers College Press.

McCormick, L., Noonan, M.J., & Heck, R. (1998). Variables affecting engagement in inclusive preschool classrooms. *Journal of Early Intervention, 21,* 160–176. doi:10.1177/105381519802100208

McWilliam, R.A. (2005). DEC recommended practices: Interdisciplinary models. In S. Sandall, M.L. Hemmeter, B.J. Smith, & M.E. McLean (Eds.), *DEC recommended practices: A comprehensive guide for practical application in early intervention/early childhood special education* (pp. 127–146). Longmont, CO: Sopris West.

Miller, P.S., & Stayton, V.D. (2005). DEC recommended practices: Personnel preparation. In S. Sandall, M.L. Hemmeter, B.J. Smith, & M.E. McLean (Eds.), *DEC recommended practices: A comprehensive guide for practical application in early intervention/early childhood special education* (pp. 189–220). Longmont, CO: Sopris West.

Oliver, C. (1990). Determinants of interorganizational relationships: Integration and future directions. *Academy of Management Review, 15*(2), 241–265. doi:10.2307/258156

Peck, C.A., Furman, G.C., & Helmstetter, E. (1993). Integrated early childhood programs: Research on the implementation of change in organizational contexts. In C.A. Peck, S.L. Odom, & D.D. Bricker (Eds.), *Integrating young children with disabilities into community programs: Ecological perspectives on research and implementation* (pp. 187–205). Baltimore, MD: Paul H. Brookes Publishing Co.

Rose, D.F., & Smith, B.J. (1993). Preschool mainstreaming: Attitude barriers and strategies for addressing them. *Young Children, 48*(4), 59–62. Reprinted in Paciorek, K.M., & Munro, J.H. (Eds.). (1994, 1995). *Early childhood education: Annual editions.* Guilford, CT: Dushkin Publishing Group.

Rous, B., & Smith, B. (2011). Key national and state policy implementation issues. In C.J. Groark (Series Ed.) & S. Eidelman (Vol. Ed.), *Early childhood intervention: Shaping the future for children with special needs and their families, three volumes: Vol. 1.* Santa Barbara, CA: ABC-CLIO, Praeger.

Sandall, S., Hemmeter, M.L., Smith, B.J., & McLean, M.E. (2005). *DEC recommended practices: A comprehensive guide for practical application in early intervention/early childhood special education.* Missoula, MT: Sopris West.

Selden, S.C., Sowa, J.E., & Sandfort J. (2006). The impact of nonprofit collaboration in early child care and education on management and program outcomes. *Public Administration Review, 66*(3), 412–425. doi:10.1111/j.1540-6210.2006.00598.x

Smith, B., & Bredekamp, S. (1998). Foreword. In L. Johnson, M. LaMontagne, P. Elgas, & A. Bauer (Eds.), *Early childhood education: Blending theory, blending practice.* Baltimore, MD: Paul H. Brookes Publishing Co.

Strain, P.S., McGee, G.G., & Kohler, F.W. (2001). Inclusion of children with autism in early intervention environments: An examination of rationale, myths, and procedures. In M. Guralnick (Ed.), *Early childhood inclusion: Focus on change* (pp. 337–364). Baltimore, MD: Paul H. Brookes Publishing Co.

Tuckman, B.W. (1965). Developmental sequence in small groups. *Psychological Bulletin, 63,* 384–399.

Wolery, R.A., & Odom, S.L. (2000). *An administrator's guide to preschool inclusion.* Chapel Hill: University of North Carolina, Frank Porter Graham (FPG) Child Development Center, Early Childhood Research Institute on Inclusion. Retrieved from http://www.fpg.unc.edu/sites/fpg.unc.edu/files/resources/reports-and-policy-briefs/ECRII_Administrators_Guide_2000.pdf

CHAPTER 7

What Are the Barriers and How Can I Address Them?

Sarika S. Gupta and Megan E. Vinh

As an early childhood administrator or program leader, you hold a powerful role in creating and maintaining an organizational culture that not only values but demands high-quality inclusive education for all preschool-age children. You are responsible for creating, informing, and driving program policy. You are most likely also accountable for ensuring that federal, state, and/or local policies and regulations are followed in your program. In this work, it is helpful to anticipate challenges. The goal of this chapter is to illuminate some of the potential roadblocks or barriers that could impede your program's progress. We present commonly reported challenges within the context of the chapters presented in this book, but we also offer potential solutions and strategies, with the hope that you will use and modify them to address the unique needs of your program, children, and families.

It is helpful to anticipate challenges.

LEARN WHAT INCLUSION MEANS AND LOOKS LIKE

Barrier: Much resistance to and obstacles surrounding inclusion revolve around individual understandings of inclusion. Although you can certainly communicate the content in Chapter 1 to your staff, consider broadening the perspectives of families and staff in several ways.

Solution: Reach out to your local OSEP-funded Parent Training and Information (PTI) center, designed to support families and parents in securing access, participation, and outcomes for children and youth with disabilities. Ask the center to compile a list of inclusion-related workshops and support groups and share it with parents and families.

Support families and parents in securing access, participation, and outcomes for children and youth with disabilities.

Solution: Work with your ILT to gather and develop materials that show staff and families what inclusion looks like in a program or classroom. One example is available at http://www.theinclusiveclass.com.

LEARN THE LAWS

Barrier: Confusion about inclusion can arise from misunderstanding the laws and requirements that govern it.

Solution: Laws are detailed and can seem intimidating. Engage experts to prepare summaries and share resources that will help your staff and families understanding inclusion. Begin with your local PTI center. They will likely advise you to use their resources or visit parent-friendly sites such as the following:

- The Arc, accessible at http://www.thearc.org/
- National Dissemination Center for Children with Disabilities (NICHCY), accessible at http://nichcy.org/
- The Parent Advocacy Coalition for Education Rights, known as the PACER Center, accessible at http://www.pacer.org/
- Wrightslaw, accessible at http://www.wrightslaw.com/

With local chapters, advocacy support, and parent-friendly information, these resources are helpful in understanding various provisions that support inclusion. (Review Chapter 2 to see IDEA's LRE provision, the Head Start Act's mandated enrollment policy regarding children with disabilities, and the ADA's accessibility guidelines.)

LEARN THE RESEARCH

Barrier: Staff and families believe inclusion benefits only some groups of children.

Solution: Summarize the research-based benefits of inclusion for children with disabilities and typically developing children. You might do this several ways:

- Survey staff and families to determine common questions. Use questions to develop a Q&A document. Draft a handout and/or post questions and research-based findings on your program's web site. Use the material in Chapter 3.
- Develop an "Inclusion Corner" in your program's newsletter to families, highlighting recent questions, concerns, and new facts/research as you learn them.
- Remember that research can be formal or informal. Ask staff and families to record quotes from children about their peers and activities that demonstrate sensitivity to others' individual learning styles and abilities. Feature these quotes and activities on your program web site or in the program or class newsletter.

ANTICIPATE BARRIERS AROUND THE ASSESSMENT OF PROGRAM READINESS

Garnering Parent and Family Support

Barrier: Parents express hesitation about inclusion.

Solution: Develop a resource library consisting of pamphlets, videos, web sites, and other information. Encourage parents to check out and review the materials.

Solution: If your program is moving to an inclusive model, partner with a program/school that is implementing high-quality inclusion. Work with the leadership to learn how to do the following:

- Organize joint parent information nights. Share with parents the expectation for inclusion and a plan to move the program in that direction.
- Develop an inclusion observation series in which parents can observe inclusion in practice then meet with administrators and teachers to ask questions about how it works.
- Partner parents in your program with parents in the inclusive program, building informal support groups.

Partner with a program/school that is implementing high-quality inclusion.

Barrier: Parents of children without disabilities support inclusion but are using inappropriate terminology to describe children with disabilities.

Solution: Educate parents about the purpose and use of person-first language (e.g., instead of "an autistic boy," say "a boy with autism"), acknowledging the individual before his or her disability. Print copies of "People-First Language" by Kathie Snow (2013) and share with parents.

Solution: In each child's enrollment package, ask each parent or family member to sign a Person-First Pledge of Respect, in which he or she agrees to use respectful, person-first language.

Barrier: Parents express resistance to inclusion.

Solution: Organize a series of events for families that address the following topics:

- *Inclusion 101.* Explain what inclusion is and is not, how inclusion "works," and what children and families should anticipate.

- *Parent and family perspectives on inclusion.* Prepare a panel of parents and families of children with and without disabilities. Ask the panel to share testimonials. Encourage attending parents to bring questions.
- *Staff perspectives on inclusion.* Invite staff to share exceptional or innovative inclusive practices, video clips and recordings from class time, and other products that demonstrate child growth and learning. Also ask staff to record 1–2 quotes from children demonstrating children's growing sensitivity to individual learning styles, abilities, and diverse backgrounds.
- *Benefits of inclusion.* Summarize research presented in Chapter 3 in parent-friendly terms. Share data on child progress.
- *Resource night.* Invite parents to share resources. You might empower parents to create and manage a "resource corner" in the program or on the program's web site. Ask them to share new resources and research-based information at meetings.

Invite staff to share exceptional or innovative inclusive practices.

Solution: In all cases, it will be helpful to develop a clear plan to communicate with and update parents on inclusion efforts. Communicate this plan to staff who may also be fielding parent/family questions and concerns. Invite staff to improve the communication plan based on parent/family needs.

Develop a clear plan to communicate with and update parents on inclusion efforts.

Garnering Staff Support

Barrier: Individuals connected to your early childhood program have negative attitudes toward individuals with disabilities. Negative or limited attitudes about any group of individuals most often stem from misinformation or lack of information. Information, exposure, and guidance are probably the most common cures.

Solution: Begin with teachers and program staff. Research informs us that attitudes toward inclusion have been linked to children's individual characteristics and the type and severity of children with special needs exhibited "rather than being rooted in a global educational placement philosophy applying equally to all types of children with special needs" (Eiserman, Shisler, & Healey 1995, p. 157). Support teaching staff to see the potential in each child.

Also address parent attitudes. Ask staff to spend the first week of school collecting information from parents and families about children's strengths, talents, and gifts (McConnell, Hubbard-Berg, & Keith, 1996). Staff may use informal conversations with parents or "get to know" activities. Use newsletters to share information about children's capabilities or celebrate shared and unique interests through photobooks and displays. Encourage staff to model for parents how to focus on children's capabilities rather than on children's limitations.

Barrier: Individuals connected to your early childhood program hold unfoundedly low expectations and/or hold the belief that children with or at risk for disabilities are ultimately limited in their capacity for growth and progress.

Solution: Staff should hold expectations for children's learning that are grounded in both a knowledge of child development and each child's current level of functioning. With this knowledge, staff can develop specific, measureable goals for guiding and supporting that child to achieve the "next steps" to scaffold and support child learning.

Solution: Use resources such as Sandall and Schwartz's (2008) *Building Blocks for Teaching Preschoolers with Special Needs Second Edition* to learn how to collect information about children's abilities and needs and then use that information to intentionally embed intervention into daily activities. When staff monitor children's interests and development, they will be more likely to see growth, or evidence that children with disabilities can make great gains. With your support, staff will also be more likely to reflect on their instruction as a way to improve child learning.

When staff monitor children's interests and development, they will be more likely to see growth, or evidence that children with disabilities can make great gains.

Barrier: "We want inclusion, but we don't have the time to plan for it!" According to Lieber and colleagues (1997), teachers cite the lack of planning time as an impediment to inclusion.

Solution: Provide planning time ahead of the school year, so teachers feel prepared rather than involved in a game of catch-up once the year starts.

Solution: Pair a novice teacher with an experienced one to encourage idea sharing and collaborative problem solving.

Solution: Provide weekly planning times for teaching teams during the school year. Also, consider planning monthly brainstorming lunches, during which various teaching teams can meet to address issues and develop solutions. Ask teams to think of 1–2 issues as well as 1–2 scenarios in which they thought they effectively met children's individual needs and how those needs were met. Such a *community of practice* will build a shared ownership for inclusion across your program.

Barrier: "We need more resources, and we don't have the training!" Resources can mean financial, physical, or staff support. Find out what staff needs are.

Solution: Create a new position—an inclusion coach—to determine where staff members need support, to provide continuous on-site mentoring, and to plan targeted professional development activities. Results from a literature review on coaching in early childhood suggest that the combination of professional development and on-site support is likely to promote teacher practices and child outcomes (Gupta & Daniels, 2012). Think about coaches as a vehicle to share new strategies, encourage teachers' review of their practices, and deliver targeted feedback that will help teachers better support children's individual needs and abilities.

Solution: Using activities in Chapters 5 and 6, build a relationship with a program that is implementing inclusion and is under the guidance of a licensed early childhood special educator. Develop an agreement with the program to allow the educator to provide supervision to teaching and family support staff at multiple sites. Alternatively, if distance and funding are issues, use concrete video coaching strategies to support teacher reflection, planning, and improvement (Powell, Diamond, Burchinal, & Kohler, 2010).

Solution: Become familiar with CONNECT: The Center to Mobilize Early Childhood Knowledge (see http://community.fpg.unc.edu). CONNECT is a free online series of modules developed to help practitioners respond to a range of challenges that may arise in diverse early childhood settings. Each module promotes practitioners' evidence-based decision-making abilities through a systematic process (CONNECT, n.d.; see Chapter 2 for a review of evidence-based practices) and includes a wealth of resources to understand how these specific practices promote outcomes in young children and their families. Module topics include *embedded interventions, transition, communication for collaboration, family–professional partnerships, assistive technology, dialogic reading practices,* and *tiered instruction,* and all are available at no cost. Perhaps most notable is the Foundations of Inclusion Training Curriculum (see http://community.fpg.unc.edu/connect-modules/instructor-community/module-1/Training-Module-on-Early-Childhood-Inclusion), a 2-hour workshop that supports practitioner understanding of policies supporting inclusion. This curriculum, along with this book, is a good way for you to strengthen your understanding of inclusion without incurring costs. You might also require all new staff to complete the 2-hour training curriculum in small groups before the school year begins. If costs are an issue, you might also ask your new inclusion coach to lead teams through modules most relevant to the challenges they are seeing in their classrooms.

Ensuring Program Readiness: Developing Program Procedures and Policies

Soon after developing your inclusion vision statement (see Chapter 6), share it far and wide. Begin by posting it in classrooms, include it in parent handbooks, display it throughout your school, and incorporate it in all program materials and communication products. Despite these initial efforts, you will recognize that much more is needed. Developing program procedures and policies that guide the practice described in the vision statement is the next step.

Soon after developing your inclusion vision statement (see Chapter 6), share it far and wide.

Barrier: There is a lack of policies, procedures, and time allotted that support and encourage collaboration among leaders, staff, specialists, and/or families.

Solution: Allocate time and resources for programwide collaborative planning and activities for the purpose of developing infrastructure that supports an integrated system of inclusive services. For leaders managing several programs, you may want to allocate time and resources across several programs.

Barrier: There is a lack of policies and procedures that support and encourage coordination of procedures, programs, personnel, and services in typical settings where children who are typically developing play, learn, and interact with children with special needs.

Solution: Early childhood administrators and leaders such as you are responsible for spearheading coordination efforts. This is where the communitywide or programwide ILT becomes essential. This group of stakeholders should be tasked with developing and executing a collaborative vision and action plan that leads to the implementation of high-quality inclusion.

Challenges to Collaboration

Barrier: Concerns from the school district or lead agency responsible for children's IEPs may emerge if children receive services in a community program that is new to inclusion. In this situation, school district administrators may be apprehensive or unsure about how to monitor the quantity and quality of services that children with disabilities are receiving.

Solution: Set up clearly defined expectations and a consistent system for communication. Develop a cohesive method of monitoring the child's progress in the community program. Offer to work with the school district administrators on reviewing the program's use of inclusive practices and the impact of these practices on child and family outcomes, especially as they pertain to goals identified in a child's IEP.

Develop a cohesive method of monitoring the child's progress in the community.

Barrier: School district administrators may wonder if a community placement for preschool children with or at risk for disabilities will be able to effectively meet the needs of these children and provide support and instruction that leads to improved outcomes.

Solution: Use recommended standards of quality to measure and strengthen the classroom environment and teachers' practices (see Chapter 4 for NAEYC accreditation standards and DEC recommended practices). You can also talk to staff and families in the community program to get a sense of their opinions on inclusion and hopefully their feelings of competence about implementing inclusion. Also remember that part of the agreement between a community-based early childhood program and the local education agency (e.g., often the local school district) should clearly describe the supplementary aides and services that will be made available to the child and/or teacher primarily responsible for that child's education. Defining exactly what these supplementary aides and services are and how they will be used to support progress toward the child's IEP goals is very important to include within the language of the IEP. The definition of what this includes is wide open to interpretation so the IEP should be designed to provide the resources and supports necessary to support the teacher, child, and family.

Barrier: Differences of opinion among ILT members emerge.

Solution: Described briefly in Chapter 6, a SWOT analysis describes a group's effort to identify *strengths, weaknesses, opportunities,* and *threats* for a shared effort (e.g., Bryson, 2004; Hayden, Frederick, & Smith, 2003; Mintzberg, 1994). Ultimately, teams conduct SWOT analyses to define shared goals and next steps. Use Form 7.1 to initiate this work. Revisit it when differences of opinion arise in order to refocus the group. Proactively, leaders might also remind team members of these components at each meeting and invite leaders to revise strengths, weaknesses, opportunities, and challenges as efforts move forward.

Solution: Create a *sticky wall* during each meeting to facilitate idea and task sharing. Sticky walls, described best by Hayden, Frederick, and Smith (2003), are visual soundboards used to facilitate idea sharing. Traditionally, group members record individual ideas and proposed tasks on index cards and then affix them to a wall, enabling group members to visually identify the common ground that team members are working from. A simple alternative to a sticky wall is a large pad of flipchart paper and Post-it notes. Whatever the strategy, the goal is to provide group members with a visual tool to brainstorm and organize their thoughts to develop an action plan. Taking pictures of sticky walls and dating them is often a helpful way to track team progress as efforts move forward. It also offers the group an informal resource of ideas to draw from as similar or new situations arise.

Provide group members with a visual tool to brainstorm and organize their thoughts to develop an action plan.

Barrier: Differences of opinion arise within a stakeholder group that includes individuals beyond your program.

Solution: Use a *nominal group process* to build consensus and ensure group member participation in meetings and efforts (Delbecq,

INCLUSION LEADERSHIP TEAM STRENGTHS, WEAKNESSES, OPPORTUNITIES, AND THREATS ANALYSIS

Strengths	Weaknesses/ needs/concerns	Opportunities	Threats/barriers/ challenges

Form 7.1. Inclusion Leadership Team Strengths, Weaknesses, Opportunities, and Threats Analysis

Van de Ven, & Gustafson, 1971). Leaders must identify a facilitator to guide this process. The process involves posing a set of open-ended questions and then, for each question, proceeding through a series of steps designed to elicit participants' insights about planning, goal setting, and/or problem solving. Leaders begin by asking stakeholders open-ended questions to first determine needs or concerns, then identify potential solutions, and finally formulate solutions. Develop several open-ended questions in advance of the meeting. Here are a couple examples:

- *Question 1:* From your perspective, what have been the specific challenges or barriers to implementing a model of full inclusion throughout our program/school/center?
- *Question 2:* From your perspective, what are some strategies or solutions that could facilitate the implementation of a model of high-quality, full inclusion throughout our program/school/center?

For each question posed, the leader will guide the group to do the following:

- Generate ideas silently, perhaps by recording responses to the question.
- Share ideas in a round-robin format in which each individual will share one idea that is posted visually (e.g., chart paper, projected on a screen, white/chalk board) without discussion or comment.
- Discuss and clarify ideas within a set amount of time, allowing participants to ask questions to understand better the ideas posted.
- Individually rank 10 items of interest or concern.
- Compare and compute how items are ranked.
- Present and discuss rankings, setting aside any non–top 10 items.
- Reorganize the top 10 through group discussion as needed.
- Ask the group to rate each item on a 7-point scale; 1 is not important and 7 is very important (Delbecq, Van de Ven, & Gustafson, 1975).

With a list of ranked tasks, the group can then begin to explore the feasibility of each task. Identifying the average importance rating for each barrier (generated from your nominal group process for Question 1) will enable to you to prioritize which of these challenges you should begin to address first. Understanding the feasibility rating of each solution (generated from your nominal group process for Question 2) will allow you to perceive the difficulty associated with implementing a particular strategy. You may choose to build momentum by starting with the implementation of some "easy win" solutions (e.g., those receiving the highest ratings of feasibility), then moving to strategies or approaches that will be likely be more challenging to undertake (e.g., those receiving lower ratings of feasibility). Rather than completing the nominal group process for both questions back to back, another option would be to complete the nominal group process only for Question 1 to begin thinking about initial barriers to full inclusion that must be addressed in your program/school/center. Once those responses are generated, ranked, and rated, the nominal group process could then be completed for Question 2 to brainstorm explicit strategies and solutions to address identified barriers in the first round.

Research using the nominal group process often produces betters "results" in terms of generating more creative ideas, strategies, and solutions among group members when compared with less structured group interactions (e.g., Kincaid, Childs, Blase, & Wallace, 2007).

FINAL THOUGHTS

Obstacles are bound to arise. Taking time individually with families, with staff, or with your ILT to anticipate barriers will help you develop a strategic plan to address any hindrances. This chapter only covers some barriers. When unique challenges arise, write them down, along with whatever action was taken to address them. This way you can document your efforts and refer back to them if similar circumstances arise. Sharing what worked with other programs experiencing similar issues is also a good way to use this information. Adapt Form 7.2 (see Figure 7.1 for filled-in example of Form 7.2) to collect the information you need to monitor your progress.

Taking time individually with families, with staff, or with your ILT to anticipate barriers will help you develop a strategic plan to address any hindrances.

ANTICIPATING AND ADDRESSING BARRIERS

Barrier	Proposed solution	Resources	Lead individual	Action taken	Follow-up or next steps

Form 7.2. Anticipating and Addressing Barriers

ANTICIPATING AND ADDRESSING BARRIERS

Barrier	Proposed solution	Resources	Lead individual	Action taken	Follow-up or next steps
A new staff member feels a child with Down syndrome is not "suited" for her class.	Explore and address staff members' attitudes about Down syndrome and/or inclusion. Pair a novice teacher with an experienced one to encourage idea sharing and collaborative problem solving. Provide weekly planning time.	Planning time, resources about Down syndrome, a mentor teacher	Me (director), mentor teacher (ideally a volunteer with inclusion experience)	Prior to the start of the school year, introduce the new staff to the mentor teacher. Provide adequate planning time both prior to and during the school year that is dedicated to individualized planning and plan to attend the first meeting.	Attend the first meeting, and share information about the child and family. Ask the new staff member in what areas she feels she needs more info and/or support. Plan next steps (e.g., establish next meeting time, locate resources, prepare mentor teacher to model individualized planning).
Differences of opinion emerge during the ILT meeting. Some staff members think that the program is not safe for a potential child with a visual impairment to attend. Other staff members contend that the program should find a way to support this child, given its inclusive mission.	Complete a SWOT analysis of the overall program to identify strengths, weaknesses, opportunities, and challenges of the physical environment. Complete a SWOT analysis of the classroom space and environment in which the child will likely be included. Use a nominal group process to ensure group participation.	Copies of SWOT forms, planning time at next ILT meeting	Me (director), facilitator of next ILT meeting	Prior to the next meeting, staff are encouraged to individually complete the SWOT form. Ask staff to bring their SWOT forms to next meeting to discuss strengths, weaknesses, opportunities, and challenges that must be considered to safely include this child in the program and the classroom.	At the end of the allotted time, rank the top 3 concerns and strategies to address those concerns. Generate a next-steps list that includes searching for resources or creative brainstorming to address concerns. Set aside time at the next meeting for the group to share ideas to address (and potentially eliminate) concerns.

Figure 7.1. Filled-in example of Form 7.2.

REFERENCES

Bryson, J.M. (2004). *Strategic planning for public and nonprofit organizations: A guide to strengthening and sustaining organizational achievement* (3rd ed.). San Francisco, CA: Jossey Bass.

CONNECT (n.d.). *CONNECT: The Center to Mobilize Early Childhood Knowledge* [fact sheet]. Retrieved from http://connect.fpg.unc.edu/

Delbecq, A.L., Van de Ven, A.H., & Gustafson, D.H. (1971). *Group techniques for program planning: A guide to nominal group and Delphi processes.* Middleton, WI: Green Briar Press. Retrieved from https://sites.google.com/a/umn.edu/avandeven/publications/research/group-techniques-for-program-planning

Eiserman, W.D., Shisler, L., & Healey, S. (1995). A community assessment of preschool providers' attitudes toward inclusion. *Journal of Early Intervention, 19*(2), 149–167.

Gupta, S.S., & Daniels, J. (2012). Coaching and professional development in early childhood classrooms: Current practices and recommendations for the future. *NHSA Dialogue, 15*(2), 206–220.

Hayden, P., Frederick, L., & Smith, B.J. (2003). *A road map for facilitating collaborative teams.* Longmont, CO: Sopris West.

Kincaid, D., Childs, K., Blase, K.A., & Wallace, F. (2007). Identifying barriers and facilitators in implementing schoolwide positive behavior support. *Journal of Positive Behavior Interventions, 9*(3), 174–184.

Lieber, J., Beckman, P.J., Hanson, M.J., Janko, S., Marquart, J.M., Horn, E., & Odom, S.L. (1997). The impact of changing roles on relationships between professionals in inclusive programs for young children. *Early Education and Development, 8*(1), 67–82. doi:10.1207/s15566935eed0801_6

McConnell, T., Hubbard-Berg, L., & Keith, D. (1996). Elementary school inclusion start-up strategies. *Inclusive Education Programs, 3*(9), 1–2.

Mintzberg, H. (1994). *The rise and fall of strategic planning.* New York, NY: Harper & Row.

Powell, D.R., Diamond, K.E., Burchinal, M., R., & Koehler, M.J. (2010). Effects of an early literacy professional development intervention on Head Start teachers and children. *Journal of Educational Psychology, 102,* 299–312. doi:10.1037/a0017763

Sandall, S.R., & Schwartz, I.S. (2008). *Building blocks for teaching preschoolers with special needs* (2nd ed.). Baltimore, MD: Paul H. Brookes Publishing Co.

Snow, K. (2013). People-first language. Retrieved from http://www.disabilityisnatural.com

APPENDIX

Frequently Asked Questions

CHAPTER 1

Q1: How do DEC and NAEYC define inclusion?

- "Early childhood inclusion embodies the values, policies, and practices that support the right of every infant and young child and his or her family, regardless of ability, to participate in a broad range of activities and contexts as full members of families, communities, and society. The desired results of inclusive experiences for children with and without disabilities and their families include a sense of belonging and membership, positive social relationships and friendships, and development and learning to reach their full potential. The defining features of inclusion that can be used to identify high quality early childhood programs and services are access, participation, and supports." (DEC/NAEYC, 2009, p. 2)

Q2: What are the three features of high-quality inclusion?

- *Access.* Children have access to all learning opportunities, activities, and experiences.
- *Participation.* Children are meaningfully included in daily routines.
- *Supports.* Infrastructure and/or programmatic supports are in place to engage families, teachers, and staff in promoting inclusion.

Q3: What does research say about early childhood inclusion?

The National Professional Development Center on Inclusion (2009) at the Frank Porter Graham Child Development Institute at the University of North Carolina at Chapel Hill synthesized the research into nine points (summarized here):

1. Inclusion takes many forms.
2. There has been some progress in efforts to ensure access to inclusive programs for children with disabilities, but universal access for all children with disabilities is far from a reality.
3. Children in inclusive programs generally do at least as well as those in specialized programs. Inclusion benefits children with and without disabilities, particularly with respect to social development.
4. Factors such as policies, resources, and beliefs influence acceptance and implementation of inclusion.
5. Specialized instruction is an important component of inclusion that affects child outcomes.

6. Collaboration among parents, teachers, and specialists is a cornerstone of high-quality inclusion.
7. Families of children with disabilities generally view inclusion favorably, though some express concern about the quality of early childhood programs and services.
8. Limited research suggests that the quality of early childhood programs that enroll young children with disabilities is as good as, or slightly better than, the quality of programs that do not. Most studies, however, have focused on general program quality, not the quality of inclusion for individual children with disabilities and their families.
9. Some evidence suggests that early childhood professionals may not be adequately prepared to serve young children with disabilities in inclusive programs.

(To see supporting references for each of these points, visit http://npdci.fpg.unc.edu.)

Q4: What is the continuum of early childhood settings?

- Settings with typical peers and inclusive services
- Settings with typical peers and separate services
- Separate settings

CHAPTER 2

Q1: What federal laws support inclusion?

- IDEA, 2004
- ADA, 1990
- Section 504 of the Rehabilitation Act of 1973
- Improving Head Start for School Readiness Act of 2007

Q2: What is the purpose of IDEA?

- IDEA establishes rights and protections for children with disabilities and their families.
- Part B of the act ensures that children ages 3–21 with disabilities have access to a FAPE.
- Part C of the act supports states in developing a system for providing early intervention services for infants and toddlers with disabilities.

Q3: How does IDEA support inclusion?

- Through the LRE provision, which states that children with disabilities are to be educated with their peers without disabilities to the maximum extent appropriate
- Through regulations stating that public agencies must ensure that a child with disabilities must be educated in the school or program he or she would attend if he or she did not have a disability unless the child's IEP requires otherwise

Q4: What are the aims of the ADA and Section 504 of the Rehabilitation Act of 1973? How do these laws support inclusion in early childhood?

- The ADA is an antidiscrimination law that protects individuals with disabilities against discrimination in a variety of contexts and settings.
- Section 504 states that qualified individuals with a disability cannot be excluded from any program or activity that receives federal financial assistance.
- Both the ADA and Section 504 safeguard access to programs and services that are federally funded and prohibit discrimination based on service availability, accessibility, and delivery.
- The ADA and Section 504 define disability more broadly, which may offer protections to children who do not qualify as having a disability under IDEA.

Q5: How does the Improving Head Start for School Readiness Act of 2007 support inclusion?

- The act supports inclusion of children with special needs in Head Start programs.
- Programs cannot deny child placement based on disability type or severity; programs must actively recruit children with disabilities.
- Staff attitudes and resource needs cannot prohibit a child with disabilities from being served in a Head Start classroom.

CHAPTER 3

Q1: Are children with disabilities being included in general early childhood settings?

- Yes, but more work is needed. See Chapter 3 for specific data.

Q2: In what ways do children with disabilities benefit from inclusion?

- Children with disabilities who are included in general education settings are more likely to exhibit positive social and emotional behaviors than their peers in segregated settings.

Q3: How important is it that children are included in the early years rather than in later grades? Is there evidence of long-term gains?

- Students enrolled in inclusion programs in their early years are likely to demonstrate socially acceptable behaviors and interactions, increased social interactions with all peers, fewer feelings of stigmatization, and academic gains via test scores and high school graduation rates.

Q4: How do typically developing children benefit from inclusion?

- More positive attitudes toward diverse peers
- Increased social skills (e.g., initiating interactions, negotiating, sharing)
- Demonstrating fairness and equity in play
- Modeling both prosocial and academic behaviors to peers with disabilities
- Becoming natural, confident leaders who are less likely to view disability as an impairment
- Increased likelihood that they will initiate friendships and assist individuals with diverse needs and qualities

Q5: What is evidence-based practice in early childhood?

- Evidence-based practice is a decision-making process both practitioners and parents should engage in to promote outcomes in young children. It relies on research, professional wisdom, and family priorities and values.

Q6: Where can I learn more about evidence-based practices that support inclusion?

- Professional journals, conferences, workshops, and local resources. Also see the specific resources listed in the chapter.

CHAPTER 4

Q1: What are the major differences between NAEYC accreditation standards and DEC recommended practices?

- The 10 NAEYC accreditation standards are an index for program quality in early childhood, whereas DEC recommended practices summarize the actions known to be effective in promoting positive outcomes. Both are supported by research.

Q2: What factors might influence programwide inclusion?

- Program administration, instruction, and what teachers do in a classroom to promote learning and development

Q3: What environmental factors should I consider before implementing inclusion?

- Classroom space, furniture, schedule and routine, centers and activities, number of adults, number of children, and ratio of adults to children

Q4: Which early childhood classroom features support social and emotional development?

- Teachers greet children upon arrival, a class schedule or routine is visible to children, group size is appropriate for age, teachers observe children's work and play, activities and areas are engaging and support learning and development in all domains, opportunities for play are available, teachers engage and respond to children, teachers guide learning and development but also follow children's interests, teachers are aware of children's diverse abilities and regard all children positively

Q5: What's the first step in preparing a program to include children with disabilities, and how does one get buy-in from busy staff?

- Improve the quality of program practices.
- Empower staff with knowledge and shared ownership in the decision-making process.

Q6: What concerns might families have about inclusion?

- Why should inclusion be implemented?
- Will my child receive an appropriate amount of attention?
- Does it promote positive outcomes in diverse populations?

Q7: How do I address the concern that inclusion may limit the academic advancement of typically developing children?

- Refer to the research in Chapter 3 that shows that all children benefit in inclusive settings. Typical peers develop self-confidence and leadership skills as they become models for their peers with disabilities.

Q8: Where can I find practical tips to help my staff include children with disabilities?

- The Head Start Center for Inclusion: http://depts.washington.edu/hscenter/
- Sandall, S.R., & Schwartz, I.S. (2008). *Building blocks for teaching preschoolers with special needs* (2nd ed.). Baltimore, MD: Paul H. Brookes Publishing Co.

CHAPTER 5

Q1: What early learning programs support children ages 3–5?

- Head Start, child care, TANF, Title I preschool, preschool special education (IDEA Part B-619), state-funded prekindergarten, private programs

Q2: Do all early learning programs for preschoolers support inclusion?

- Even though all early learning programs share a collective aim of supporting young children, they may differ in the way they accomplish this aim. Knowing the purpose, aims, and eligibility requirements of your program will help you understand how young children with disabilities should be supported and included.

Q3: How are the ADA and Section 504 of the Rehabilitation Act of 1973 relevant to my early childhood program?

- Both prevent discrimination against children with disabilities in any public setting.

Q4: Where can I find resources to help me understand the inclusion requirements in my early learning program?

- See Chapter 5 for resources to help you understand how IDEA, Section 504, and the ADA have an impact on your early learning program.

CHAPTER 6

Q1: How can I describe collaboration clearly to my staff to engage them in the process?

- Collaboration is teamwork. Teamwork involves exchanging understanding and expertise. Use teamwork to build a shared commitment.

Q2: What are the benefits of collaboration?

- Inclusion is more likely to be successful, and children are more likely to experience the benefits described in Chapter 3 when professionals collaborate.

Q3: What steps should I keep in mind to ensure my team is collaborative?

- Offer opportunities to build trust and to develop a shared goal. Anticipate potential barriers to manage the process efficiently, effectively, and positively.

Q4: What is an *inclusion leadership team* and who should be involved?

- Also known as an ILT, the team includes individuals who will work together to implement and sustain high quality inclusion

Q5: Should I expect the ILT to operate smoothly throughout the year?

- A team will grow and develop over time. Individuals are likely to begin in the *forming phase,* remaining polite but guarded. As members identify a common goal, they will likely identify differing perspectives, moving into the *storming phase.* At times, the team may feel stuck, but with good leadership the team will organize an action plan, thereby moving the team into the *norming phase.* Leaders should encourage member feedback and problem-solving strategies. The *performing phase* follows as the team begins to implement its action plan. The team will likely move back and forth through the stages, ideally building collegiality, or it can also revisit the purpose, action plan, and even membership (Hayden et al., 2003).

Q6: How should I prepare for the first ILT meeting?

- The first meeting is critical and will set the tone for future activities. The goal is to establish a trusting, collaborative, and efficient environment. Develop an agenda, plan activities, and draft guiding questions to develop a shared vision statement. Promote respectful communication and cultivate a commitment. See the following question and the chapter for a suggested time line for this work.

Q7: What is a realistic time line for the team's work?

- Ideally, teamwork should be continuous; however, for those just beginning a collaborative process, teamwork will take time. Chapter 6 outlines a 1-year action plan to help develop a pilot inclusion program that will inform the team's efforts moving forward.

Q8: How do we keep track of our efforts as a team?

- Refer back to the action plan and measure progress. Make sure efforts align with the shared vision and goals. Clarify roles and expectations for each team member and task. Revisit the action plan routinely to ensure the team is on track.

CHAPTER 7

Q1: What potential roadblocks might a program encounter as it begins inclusion efforts?

- *Lack of knowledge.* Individuals may not understand what inclusion is, how it looks, how it benefits children, and that it is guided by federal law.
- *Attitude.* Staff and parents may have negative attitudes or low expectations toward individuals with disabilities.
- *Resources.* Inclusion requires adequate time, training, collaboration, planning, and idea sharing to be successful.
- *Support.* Program policies may not support inclusion. Administrators may feel their programs and staff are not adequately equipped to support children with disabilities.
- *Familiarity.* Leaders and administrators may be unfamiliar with child development or disabilities and may not feel comfortable taking responsibility for children with disabilities.
- *Collaboration.* Differences of opinion are likely to emerge.

Q2: What are some strategies to proactively address barriers?

- See Chapter 7 for strategies to address the barriers described in the previous FAQ response.

Q2: What free, online resource provides a 2-hour Foundations of Inclusion Training Curriculum and models evidence-based decision making to address potential barriers in inclusive settings?

- CONNECT: The Center to Mobilize Early Childhood Knowledge (see http://community.fpg.unc.edu/)

Index

Figures, tables, blank forms, and notes are indicated by the letter *f, t, b,* and *n,* respectively.